101 More Music Games
for Children

Other SmartFun Books:

101 Music Games for Children by Jerry Storms
101 More Music Games for Children by Jerry Storms
101 Dance Games for Children by Paul Rooyackers
101 More Dance Games for Children by Paul Rooyackers
101 Movement Games for Children by Huberta Wiertsema
101 Drama Games for Children by Paul Rooyackers
101 More Drama Games for Children by Paul Rooyackers
101 Improv Games for Children by Bob Bedore
101 Language Games for Children by Paul Rooyackers
101 Life Skills Games for Children by Bernie Badegruber
101 More Life Skills Games for Children by Bernie Badegruber
101 Cool Pool Games for Children by Kim Rodomista
101 Family Vacation Games by Shando Varda
101 Relaxation Games for Children by Allison Bartl
101 Pep-Up Games for Children by Allison Bartl
101 Quick-Thinking Games + Riddles for Children by Allison Bartl
404 Deskside Activities for Energetic Kids by Barbara Davis, MA, MFA
Yoga Games for Children by Danielle Bersma and Marjoke Visscher
The Yoga Adventure for Children by Helen Purperhart
The Yoga Zoo Adventure by Helen Purperhart
Yoga Exercises for Teens by Helen Purperhart
101 Circus Games for Children by Paul Rooyackers

Ordering

Trade bookstores in the U.S. and Canada, please contact:

Publishers Group West
1700 Fourth Street, Berkeley CA 94710
Phone: (800) 788-3123   Fax: (800) 351-5073

Hunter House books are available at bulk discounts for course adoptions;
to qualifying community, health care, and government organizations;
and for special promotions and fund-raising. For details please contact:

Special Sales Department
Hunter House Inc., PO Box 2914, Alameda CA 94501-0914
Phone: (510) 865-5282   Fax: (510) 865-4295
E-mail: ordering@hunterhouse.com

Individuals can order our books from most bookstores,
by calling toll-free **(800) 266-5592**, or from our
website at **www.hunterhouse.com**

101 MORE
Music Games
FOR
Children

New Fun and Learning with Rhythm and Song

Jerry Storms

Translated by Amina Marix Evans &
Illustrated by Jos Hoenen

a Hunter House SmartFun book

First published in the Netherlands in 1997 by Panta Rhei as
Honderd Nieuwe Muziekspelen

Hunter House Inc., Publishers
PO Box 2914
Alameda CA 94501-0914

Library of Congress Cataloging-in-Publication Data
Storms, Ger.
[Honderd nieuwe muziekspelen. English]
101 more music games for children : new fun and learning with rhythm and song
/ Jerry Storms.
    p. cm. — (A Hunter House SmartFun book)
Includes index.
ISBN-13: 978-0-89793-298-1   ISBN-10: 0-89793-298-6
1. Games with music. 2. Music—Instruction and study. I. Title: One hundred one
    more music games for children. II. Title: One hundred and one more music
    games for children. III. Title. IV. Series.
MT948 .S8313 2000
372.87'044—dc21   00-040940

Project Credits

Cover Design and Book Production:
  Jil Weil
Book Design: Hunter House
Copy Editors: Mimi Kusch, Alexandra
  Mummery, Emily Tryer, Kiran Rana
Proofreader: Michelle Ho
Consultants: Douglas Goodkin,
  Skye Atman
Acquisitions Editor: Jeanne Brondino
Associate Editor: Alexandra Mummery

Editorial and Production Assistant:
  Emily Tryer
Publicity Manager: Sara Long
Sales and Marketing Assistant:
  Earlita K. Chenault
Customer Service Manager:
  Christina Sverdrup
Order Fulfillment: Richard Simpson
Administrator: Theresa Nelson
Computer Support: Peter Eichelberger
Publisher: Kiran S. Rana

Printed and Bound by Bang Printing, Brainerd, Minnesota
Manufactured in the United States of America

9 8 7 6 5 4   First Edition   10 11 12 13 14

Contents

A detailed list of the games indicating appropriate
age groups begins on the next page.

List of Games

	Young children	Older children	Teenagers	All ages

Expression and Improvisation Games

Rhythm Games

List of Games, continued

List of Games, continued

Preface

This book contains one hundred and one new suggestions for games based on music and sound and is divided into ten categories. It is both a sequel to and a further development of the original book, *101 Music Games for Children*. It is a sequel in that it offers new forms of games; it is a further development because in many of these new games, the accent lies more on the basics of music rather than on the social and creative aspects, which were the focus of *101 Music Games for Children*. Along with the familiar categories such as listening, concentration, and expression games, this book also includes types of games that primarily belong in the category of musical education, such as the sound games, rhythm games, game projects, and card and board games. In general, the games combine social, creative, and musical education.

The great international success of *101 Music Games for Children* is proof of the interest in this type of material: games that can be used by teachers and group leaders in all types of education and youth work. No specific musical background or ability is required for using this book, just experience in working with groups. These games are designed for use in groups; most of them can be used in classes of up to thirty participants. In only a few cases are smaller groups recommended, and this is clearly indicated in the instructions.

Many of these games were developed and tried out during music courses: creative music weeks as well as extracurricular activities for primary school teachers, music teachers, and creative therapists. Some of the games are musical variations on existing (nonmusical) games, and a number of them were especially created for this collection.

The basic arrangement of the book is comparable with that of *101 Music Games for Children* as far as the descriptions and categorization of the games are concerned: they are as practical, concrete, and clear as possible. A teacher or group leader should be able to begin working with the games without previous preparation. The most important prerequisites are the conviction that play has important educational value, a great deal of enthusiasm, and the courage to try out new activities in the class or with a group, where the results may not always be predictable.

Since this book is not exclusively for school use but also for activities such as sociocultural work and creative therapy, the terms "teacher" and "leader" are completely interchangeable. I also use the words "class," "players," and "children" interchangeably.

Jerry Storms
The Netherlands

Introduction

The Aim of the Games

All the games in this book have educational value; they are not intended simply to keep children busy. With these games, we aim to achieve three important pedagogical aims:

- social education
- creative education
- musical education

Most of the games combine these three goals, although the emphasis varies according to category. In the listening, concentration, dance and movement, and intercultural games, the social aspect is the primary focus, with the musical and creative aspects taking second place. The musical and creative aspects are the focus in the expression, sound and rhythm, game projects, and card and board games. Here the social side takes a back seat.

However, within any single category the emphasis may lie in different areas. The teacher or leader can also influence the educational value of a game by, for instance, placing more emphasis on the process and the debriefing (social education) or on the result, which improves as the game is better rehearsed (musical education). In short, most of the games develop social, creative, and musical skills in varying degrees. This mix was one of the criteria for choosing the games.

Other criteria were clear rules, excitement, humor, challenge, surprise, and cooperation rather than competition. The point of the games is not to learn musical techniques or to perform existing songs, pieces of music, or dances. As such, it makes no difference how musical the participants are or whether they play an instrument, although through playing the games they will develop many musical skills such as spontaneous singing; learn about all kinds of instruments; think up, play, and recognize all sorts of rhythms; structure sounds; familiarize themselves with written music; and so on.

The Educational Value of the Games

The games in this book also act as a counterbalance to an overdose of performance orientation. In our society, games are almost exclusively oriented toward winning: getting the highest score, giving the best individual performance, beating the opponent. Competition has always existed and need not always be seen as negative. It can encourage individuals to give spectacular performances, which in themselves have merit. However, it can also produce "losers," children who are less strong, less quick, less clever, and who do not always know how to handle losing appropriately.

Outside school, children are confronted almost exclusively with competitive games. To compensate for this, schools should emphasize noncompetitive games. It is frequently thought that competition is the only motivation for playing a game. For many people this is true; they are only prepared to take part in a game if they can win something or beat an opponent. Many traditional noncompetitive children's games such as hopscotch or jumping (skipping) rope are being replaced by competitive computer and TV games that are totally geared toward winning. Teachers and youth workers can offer children a counterbalance in the form of games that don't emphasize winning and losing—games that are exciting but also require cooperation or collective resourcefulness and are about listening to one another and working together, characteristics that are probably much more important in later life than the ability to perform well individually. Although a number of competitive games are also included in this book—since it is hard to motivate some people any other way—the emphasis in most of the games is clearly on solidarity, forming groups, cooperation, and ingenuity. The development of these characteristics is something to which expressive subjects such as music, art, dance, and drama lend themselves perfectly. Through pleasure and humor, unhappy experiences such as fear of failure, competition, discrimination, and frustration about losing can be avoided with this type of game. Whether the goals mentioned can actually be realized depends largely on how often these forms of play are presented: practice makes perfect!

Who Are These Games For?

In principle these games can be used in any group situation involving children, including elementary schools, special schools, junior high, and high schools. They are also very well suited for youth work, institutional work, creative therapy, and as a part of basic music training.

Elementary School

The games indicated for the 5-to-9 age group are mainly intended for students in elementary schools. The age group recommendation is an approximation, and teachers are free to use their own judgment in this respect. These games are not intended to replace any existing curriculum, although they can supplement and bring a little variation to it. The games can also provide a basic elementary musical foundation, as long as they are used regularly.

The games can be used systematically to increase their educational value considerably. This may be done by playing the same game three times: first as described in the book, under the supervision of a teacher; the second time under the supervision of a pupil; and a third time with a variation agreed on by the group itself (for instance, with a self-made sound drawing or score).

These games do not require any special musical skills on the part of the teacher. Most of them involve simple musical instruments and a sound installation, but the majority of schools will already have these. There is therefore no reason why you should not do something with music!

Middle School and High School

The games for the 10-to-16 age group can be used as part of the music lessons for middle school and the first two years of high school. Here again, the games should not replace any particular teaching method, but integrating the games into existing music lessons can be valuable. One of these benefits is to encourage students to work independently. This is where these games can really make a difference. Those games that require creativity on the students' part develop initiative, spontaneity, and resourcefulness and offer the students the opportunity to present themselves with something they have thought up and developed independently.

This process is intensified if the games are used methodically, as described above. In addition, since these games create a playful and safe framework, fear of failure, competition, and discrimination rarely come into play.

Youth Work

Those games in which the accent is on social education are particularly well suited for use in youth work. Here again no musical background is required. Depending on the age group, one can choose from listening games, concentration games, dance and movement games, relaxation games, intercultural games, and game projects. These games can be used during recreation periods, at day or overnight camps, in youth work, and in organizations such as Girl and Boy Scouts.

Activity Groups and Creative Therapy

The simpler games for the younger age groups in which the accent is on social education are particularly suitable as activities in institutions for special needs children and for creative therapy. There are no absolute norms to which the children need to adhere; since they do not really need to be able to keep a rhythm or to sing in tune, the children can derive a great deal of pleasure from playing these games at their own level. Games that would work particularly well in this context are the listening, concentration, expression, and sound games for the youngest age group. The games can, of course, be further simplified to suit the needs of a particular group.

Information for the Leader

The Role of the Leader

Although the most important feature of the games in this book is that they are simple and can be played by anyone, the role of the leader should not be underestimated. The leader is organizer, observer, a source of inspiration, and an umpire. Here are several points to which special attention should be paid:

- The leader should gather in advance the materials necessary for playing the game chosen (instruments, sound equipment, cassettes or CDs, papers, cards, or a drawing on the blackboard).
- The space should be suitably prepared. Do you need to push back the chairs or arrange them in a circle? Is there enough space for a movement game? Is the floor clean enough for people to lie down?
- Before starting, go through the game in your mind. The rules should be concise and conveyed clearly in a relaxed tone; it can be very helpful if while you are explaining the game you provide an example of how the game would go in which you name some of the children present for possible roles.
- The most important thing is the leader's enthusiasm. Show how much you like the game and repeatedly encourage the children during it. The leader should be a constant source of inspiration.
- If necessary, the leader may have to act as umpire and stop the game immediately if it threatens to get out of hand. Decide what you want to do if someone does not play by the rules. Watch the group closely so that you can give an unbiased opinion at any time.
- Ensure that you always have an alternative game in reserve in case the game you planned is obviously unsuitable for the group. Keep in mind that a game can work well with one group and be quite unsuitable for another. Consider the particular group in advance and whether the game you have chosen is appropriate. For instance, a hyperactive group needs more preparation for a relaxation game. With such a group you would first have to discuss the game and have their complete agreement to try it out.
- Remember that some games involve a considerable amount of noise: make sure that this will not disturb anyone, and if necessary choose a quieter game.
- Leaders should always begin by leading the game themselves. Once the game is well under way, one of the pupils can take over; this practice is strongly recommended because it increases the children's involvement in the game, and many of the games lend themselves particularly well to it.

- If a game requires multiple activities on the part of the leader, it is better not to join in. Only if after the explanation everything is self-evident can the leader take part as a member of the group: it can be great fun for the participants if they can play with the teacher on an equal footing.
- In a debriefing after a game, first point out the things that went well, including discoveries made by the children during the game. There will always be something positive to say, no matter what happened. Praise the children involved without comparing them with the others; this will motivate them to do even better next time.

About the Rules

- Never begin a game until all the participants understand the rules completely. Wait until everyone is settled in their places before you begin the explanation, and make sure that everyone is paying attention when you explain the game.
- The explanation should not be interrupted by questions or remarks; make time after the explanation for questions.
- The rules can be flexible. You may find a certain rule will prove unworkable with your group, so don't be afraid of changing a rule to suit the situation. The rules given here should not be taken as commandments.
- Remain open to suggestions from participants for adapting the rules, and incorporate them if you feel they will improve the game. These suggestions are, after all, creative contributions to the game. Any new rules should not, of course, alter the purpose of the game or create inequality between players.
- The games in this book can also be seen as a source of inspiration for your own ideas. For each game there are countless possible variations, so don't hesitate to revise the games to suit the preferences of the group or the circumstances.

Information about the Games

The one hundred and one music games in this book are divided into ten categories. Each category begins with brief information about the characteristics of the games in that group. The games are not arranged in any particular order within the categories. There is no particular method for choosing games, so leaders can rely entirely on their own preferences.

- listening games
- concentration games
- expression games
- rhythm games
- sound games
- dance and movement games
- relaxation games
- intercultural games
- game projects
- card and board games

Instruments

Most of the games require simple musical instruments, such as glockenspiels, vibraphones, xylophones, hand drums, tambourines, shakers, woodblocks, triangles, chime bars, maracas, claves, and so forth (see the figure on page 11).

If possible there should be an instrument for each participant, but for most of the games this is not essential. There are also a number of games in which only a few instruments are used at any one time. The number of instruments needed is indicated at the beginning of each game, as are any other materials that may be required.

Songs

A number of games use songs, or parts of songs. For instance, certain sounds or sequences of letters may be sung to a familiar tune, or the rhythms of well-known songs are clapped or played. In general, traditional children's songs are used, such as "Baa Baa Black Sheep," "Frère Jacques," and "Three Blind Mice." However, you don't need to use the songs mentioned; you can always substitute other nursery rhymes or modern songs if they are more familiar to the group you are working with. Sometimes you will be using only the melody or the rhythm, so the children don't need to know all the words.

Music

For the dance and movement and relaxation games, although we have provided general suggestions about genre, tempo, or type of music, you should feel free to substitute music that is more suited to your group or your own style.

For the rest of the games, feel completely free to use music from your own collections or from the local audio library. "Golden oldies" always work, as do inspiring pieces of classical music. The children don't need to know the music in advance; the important thing is that the music inspires them to participate in a creative dance game or an imaginative drawing.

The Ten Best Games

Based on my experience, the following games are the children's favorites:

1. Symphony of Syllables (listening game)

2. Living Memory (listening game)

3. Watch Out for Your Number! (concentration game)

4. The Sounding Space (expression game)

5. The Secret Rhythm (rhythm game)

6. The Tree of Sound (sound game)

7. The Car Dance (dance and movement game)

8. Head Seeks Tummy (relaxation game)

9. The Multicultural Circle Dance (intercultural game)

10. Circus Project (music project)

Key to the Icons Used with the Games

To help you find games suitable for a particular occasion and group, the games are coded using symbols or icons. These icons tell you at a glance the following things about the game:
- the appropriate age group
- the amount of time needed
- the number of instruments needed
- the props and materials required
- the space required

These are explained in more detail below.

Suitability in terms of age. These indicate the difference between games for young children, older children, teenagers, and people of all ages.

 = Young children (ages 6 to 9)

 = Older children (ages 9 to 12)

 = Teenagers (12 and up)

 = All ages

How Long the Game Takes. The games are divided into those that require about 5 minutes, 10 minutes, 20 minutes, 30 minutes, 40 minutes, and those that take 1 hour or more.

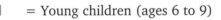

5 minutes   10 minutes   15 minutes   20 minutes

30 minutes   40 minutes   1 hour
                          or more

How many instruments you will need (if any). Many games require the use of one or more instruments.

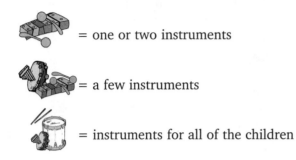

= one or two instruments

= a few instruments

 = instruments for all of the children

Whether or not you will need to prepare anything in advance. Some games require props (such as blindfolds), other materials (such as paper and pens), prepared game pieces, or recorded music (and a way to play it).

 = props, materials, prepared game pieces, recorded music

Whether you will need a large amount of space

= large space

Some of the Instruments

bongos

tambourine

maracas

xylophone

castanets

claves

glockenspiel

two-tone drum

shaker

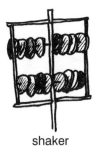

guïro

drum

triangle

chime bar

woodblock

hand drum

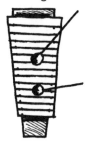

metallophone

Listening Games

The ability to listen and concentrate is an important part of every learning process. The development of these two skills is the first step on the road to social, creative, and musical education. This new collection of music games therefore includes a large number of listening and concentration games. They are comparable to the listening and concentration games found in *101 Music Games for Children*.

There are various levels of listening games. Some are very simple and mainly concerned with the recognition of sounds. These are particularly suitable for beginning work with a group. Others demand more listening skills and require distinguishing between musical characteristics (for example, in Odd Man Out). If these games are played repeatedly, the participants will get better and better, and the experience of developing listening skills will be an important part of the group's musical education.

Special Features

- The simplest games are concerned with the recognition and/or imitation of noises and sounds.
- The more difficult games are concerned with becoming familiar with musical parameters such as the pitch of a note, length of note, sound color, tempo, and so on.
- These games are active listening exercises that require a reaction or imitating something. The participants learn to listen well enough to ensure the success of the game.

Odd
Man Out

Age group: all ages. The game can be kept very simple for young children and made a little more complicated for older children; unlimited number of participants

Requirements: a few melodic instruments and a drum

The leader plays three sounds, one of which does not fit with the others, since two of the sounds share similar characteristics and the third does not. These three sounds should have a particular musical characteristic such as pitch, length of sound, sound color, rhythm, melody, tempo, and so forth. The participants have to guess which of the three sounds is different from the others and therefore the "odd man out."

Examples:

pitch: the leader plays two high notes on a melodic instrument and one low note: the low note is odd man out

duration: the leader plays two long notes and one short one

sound color: two notes are played on a glockenspiel, one on a xylophone

rhythm: two similar rhythmic patterns and one with a slightly different rhythm are played on a drum

melody: the leader plays two cheerful songs and one sad one

tempo: the leader plays two fast songs and one slow one, and so on

Young

Melody
or Rhythm?

Age group: 6–8; not too large a group

Requirements: plenty of melody and rhythm instruments

The group sits in two rows that face each other: the children in one
row have only melodic instruments, and those in the other row
have only rhythm instruments.

This game is a musical version of Simon Says. The leader plays
three different instruments in a row. If he plays a melodic instrument, the row with the melodic instruments have to play something. If someone with a rhythm instrument plays, she is out and
has to stop playing.

If the leader plays a rhythm instrument, the row with the
rhythm instruments has to play. Anyone playing a melodic instrument is out. If the leader plays another type of instrument (with
neither melody nor rhythm), for example, a cymbal or bells, then
no one should play, and anyone who does is out. Gradually
increase the pace of the game.

3

Follow My Leader

Age group: all ages; unlimited number of participants

The participants sit in a circle with their eyes closed. The leader walks around and makes sounds in three or four different places using various objects in the room, for example, by banging on the radiator, drawing the curtains, opening and closing a cupboard door or drawer, writing on the blackboard, and so on. When the leader comes back to her place the participants open their eyes and are asked who can make the same sounds in the same order. Then the participants can take turns making three or four sounds themselves, which the others have to repeat.

4

Young

What Animal Was That?

Age group: 6–8

Requirements: a blindfold

The children sit in a circle, and one of them is blindfolded. The teacher points to another child, who stands in the center of the circle; this child makes an animal sound of his own choice, for example, barking like a dog, growling like a lion, and so on.

The blindfolded child has to guess who made the sound. If she can't, the sound is repeated until the blindfolded player gets the name right. Then another child is blindfolded, and the teacher picks someone else to stand in the center and make an animal sound.

5

Young   Older

Symphony of Syllables

Age group: 6–10; unlimited number

One child leaves the room while the others sit in a circle. The group thinks of a word of two, three, or four syllables. (With younger children begin with a simple two-syllable word such as "Sunday." With older children you can use three- or four-syllable words like "November" or "Cinderella").

Each child is given a syllable. For example, child number one gets "no," child two, "vem," child three, "ber," and so on, around the entire circle. Now all the children sing their syllable at the same time to the tune of a well-known song, "Three Blind Mice," for instance. The child who was outside now enters the room and listens to the singing. Can she guess the word being used?

If the child has difficulty guessing, after a while tell her how many syllables the word has.

6

Older **Teens**

The Wolf and the Lamb

Age group: 8 and older

Requirements: 2 blindfolds; 2 instruments

The children sit or stand in a large circle. Two players stand in the center, each with an instrument, such as a tambourine and a triangle. Each of them works out her own short rhythm. Then they are blindfolded. The player with the larger instrument is the wolf, the other the lamb. The wolf has to catch the lamb by tagging her. Since they can't see each other, they have to listen for each other. The wolf plays his rhythm first, and the lamb must answer with her rhythm.

The wolf and the lamb keep moving around in small steps. If they bump into the children in the circle, those in the circle should steady them and gently guide them back to the center. Once the wolf tags the lamb, two other children become wolf and lamb. If it takes too long for the lamb to be caught, you can decide that the wolf should play only five times. If he hasn't caught the lamb by then, the lamb wins.

All Ages

Musical Guessing Game

Age group: all age groups

Requirements: 10 different instruments

The leader puts ten or more different instruments on a table in front of her, covered with a cloth. Each instrument should have a distinctive sound. One child stands with his back to the class. The leader uncovers the instruments and plays something on three of them. The listener then turns around and points out the instruments that were played. With older children you can play four or five instruments one after the other. After the leader has given an example, one of the children can take over. This is a very good game for learning the names of instruments!

8

Young   Older

Repetition Game

Age group: 6–10; maximum 20 players

Requirements: 20-bar xylophone-type instruments for each player

The children form pairs and sit opposite one another at small tables. Each child has a glockenspiel, metallophone, or xylophone, but their instruments have to remain hidden from the other child, so you can make a screen down the middle of the table (using large books standing up) or the children can put the instrument on their laps so their partners cannot see which note they are playing.

With small children just use the notes C, D, E, F, and G, with the other notes removed or covered up. Agree on which child will begin. The first child plays one note on his instrument. The other child then tries to play the same note on her instrument. She has only one chance—there are no tryouts! If the second child plays the right note, she gets a point. Then they switch, and the other child has a chance to score a point. This is done five times. Repeat the game until everyone has five points.

Now add one note to each instrument, the A, so we now have C, D, E, F, G, and A. Then the game begins again until everyone has six points. Then add the B, and finally high C.

Variation: Begin with three notes (C, D, and E). Each child plays a short melody, which her partner repeats.

9

Young

Telegraph Game

Age group: 6–9

In this game a message is passed down a long "telegraph wire," which is a long row of children standing side-by-side or in a big circle.

The first child thinks up a short rhythmic pattern and claps it; the second child repeats it, and so on to the end of the line. One child is asked in advance to create a disturbance by walking up and down the line clapping a different rhythm. The child at the end of the line checks the rhythm he claps to see if it is the same as the original rhythm. If it is, he becomes number one and begins another round with a new rhythm. The leader picks another child to create the disturbance. If the rhythm does not reach the end of the line correctly, that same rhythm should be started again from the beginning.

Young

Instrument Quiz

Age group: 6–9

Requirements: instruments for at least half the group; paper

Write all the participants' names on cards—one name on each card. The instruments should be placed behind a screen (or on the floor behind a table laid on its side). Distribute the cards more or less evenly among the instruments.

One child goes behind the screen, chooses an instrument, reads out the name on one of the cards, and plays something on the instrument. The child whose name was called out has to try and name the instrument. If she is correct, it is her turn to choose an instrument, read out a name, play something on the instrument, and so on. If she is wrong, the first child repeats the process with another instrument and another card. The game continues until everyone has had a turn.

Older

Living Memory

Age group: 8–12

Requirements: an instrument for each child

The children form pairs. One pair leaves the room, and the rest are given instruments. Pairs don't have to play the same instrument. The children with instruments now become "cards" in a game of Living Memory. Each pair now works out a rhythm or musical motif that they can both play in exactly the same way. Each pair should, of course, have its own motif.

Now the pairs split up and everyone in the group mingles, forming a big circle facing outward. The pair who left comes back into the room and stands in the middle of the circle. At a signal from the leader, all the children start to play their instruments, repeating their pattern over and over.

Just as in the card game Memory, one of the players in the middle "turns over a card" by tapping one of the musicians on the shoulder. This "card" turns round to face the center and continues playing. The player in the middle listens carefully and tries to remember or guess who is the musician's partner. The player should make his guess final by tapping the chosen musician on the shoulder. If he guesses right, this pair of "cards" stops, and the player in the middle turns over a new "card." If he guesses wrong, the two "cards" turn to face outward again and continue playing, and the other player in the middle has a turn.

Older

The Chime Bar Game

Age group: 8–10; small groups

Requirements: a chime bar (also called resonator bells) for each child

This game can be played in small groups of as many children as there are instruments, while the other children wait their turn. At least eight different notes, that is, a complete octave, should be used in this game.

Each child is given a chime bar and mallet to hit it with. The children walk slowly around the room playing and listening to one another. At a signal from the leader they form a line, keeping to the correct order of the scale. This means they have to hear which notes are higher or lower and form a line that goes from high note to low. (It is not absolutely necessary for the scale to be complete). Once the line is formed, let someone play the scale and see if it's right. Then another group can take over and try the same thing. Which group formed a correct scale the quickest? Agree beforehand where in the room the line should be formed.

Note: If real chime bars are not available, you can take eight bars from a xylophone or vibraphone and suspend them on strings.

13

Young

The Chain of Sound

Age group: 6–9 years

The children sit in a circle. The leader thinks up two random sounds, for example, whistling and buzzing. He takes the hand of the child on his left and whistles. Then he takes the hand of the child on his right and buzzes. The children then pass the sound on in the same way that they received it and in the same direction.

Sometimes the two sounds reach one child at the same time. If this happens, that child thinks up two new sounds and passes them on to her right and left in the same way that the leader began the game. If the sounds do not collide at one player, they will return to the leader, who then begins two new sounds in the same way.

14

Teens

Bird Call

Age group: 12–16; up to 20 players

Requirements: Blindfolds for each player

Divide the group into pairs. Each pair agrees on a "call," that is, a special sound or series of sounds made with the voice by which the children can recognize one another and that no one else is using. First let everyone listen to all the call notes, then blindfold all the players. Move them around the room so that they do not know where their partners are.

At a signal from the leader the players all begin using their calls, carefully making their way toward their partners. When the children find their partners, they can remove their blindfolds.

Concentration Games

The games in this section are, in general, a little more difficult than the listening games, because in addition to good listening capabilities they require the players to engage in a musical activity. The players may have to stay very quiet or make very exact sounds for the game to work.

These games require a high degree of attentiveness and observation. For this reason, some of them may be experienced as difficult or tiring, a good reason for limiting the duration. Recording the games on a cassette recorder can increase the players' attention and motivation considerably.

Musical instruments play an important role in most of these games, so it is wise to ensure that the children are familiar with the instruments before beginning the games.

Special Features

- These games require a quiet space.
- The group must be capable of attentiveness and good discipline, otherwise the games will not work.
- Most video games require a lot of concentration, which is why we have included a "living video game" with the same characteristics as a real video game: close attention to the progress of the game, the need to react quickly and adequately, the catastrophic result of mistakes, and last, the fact that the possibility of winning increases motivation.

Young

The Mosquito

Age group: 6–8

The whole class imitates the buzzing of a mosquito: bzzzzzzzzzzz.

One pupil stands in front of the class and with his arms mimics the flight of the mosquito: up, down, up, down, around in circles, and so on. This part should be done very quietly. The class follows the movements by adjusting the pitch of the buzz. When their arms go up, so does the buzz; when their arms go down, the buzz goes down. If the "mosquito" lands on a student's arm, the rest of the class is silent.

This continues until someone in the class slams their hand loudly on the table: the mosquito has been squashed, and everyone is quiet.

Young

Sound Game

Age group: 6–9

The children stand or sit in a circle. Each person thinks up a sound he can make with his voice. The leader begins with a sound such as "hoo," "sss," or "tak-a-tak-a-tak." The child on her right then makes his own sound, and so on, around the circle. In the next round the tempo is increased and in the following round, decreased.

After a few rounds, the sounds are sent around in the other

Older **Teens**

Who Is the Conductor?

Age group: 8 and older

Requirements: instruments for all the players

This is a well-known game that can be played in various ways. The players, each of whom has an instrument, stand in a circle. One child leaves the room for a moment. The leader picks another child to be the conductor. The children agree on a secret sign that the conductor will give for everyone to start and stop playing at the same time. This might be a wink or a movement of a finger or foot. The group must keep a constant eye on the conductor, who is part of the circle, without it being obvious.

The child who left the room comes back in and stands in a position from which she can observe the whole group. The group then plays and stops, following the signal they have agreed on a few times, and the observer watches closely to see if she can discover who the conductor is.

With each subsequent round, a new signal must be agreed on. There can also be signs for playing louder or softer, faster or slower, drums only or jingling instruments only, and so on. This game requires good concentration on the part of the players, because they cannot openly watch the conductor.

Variation without instruments: In this version of the game the conductor mimes instruments the group should "play," also in mime. He might begin, for example, with piano playing, then switch to violin, flute, or drums.

Young

Watch Out for Your Number!

Age group: 6–9

Each child thinks of an animal sound. The players then choose a number between one and eight, making sure to remember it.

The leader now counts slowly from one to eight, and each child makes her animal sound when her number is called. If her sound is "moo," and her number is five, when the leader calls out five, the child says "moo." Depending on the size of the group, there may be several different noises at the same time: that's part of the fun!

In the first round the leader counts out loud. The second time the numbers are played only on a drum. After a few rounds, if everyone reacts on time, the tempo can be gradually increased.

Variation: Draw a horizontal line on the board, divide it into eight equal segments and number them one to eight. Now let each child draw a small block on the line above the number she has chosen. The block represents her chosen sound. If two children choose the same number the blocks should be drawn above one another. Now perform this "score" as above.

Young

Who's Got It?

Age group: 6–8

Requirements: a tambourine

The children sit or stand in a circle. The teacher gives one child a tambourine (or anything that jingles when moved). This child chooses a classmate to stand in the middle of the circle with his eyes closed. The children in the circle all have their hands behind their backs. The child with the instrument stands outside the circle. This is a musical version of "A-Tisket, A-Tasket" in which the children in the circle sing the song:

**A-tisket, a-tasket
a green and yellow basket
I took some music to my love
and on the way I lost it.**

During the singing, the child with the instrument skips around the circle, jingling loudly. Just before the song finishes, she puts the instrument into the hands of one of the children in the circle. The child in the center has to listen very carefully to hear when the jingling stops, because when the song is over he must guess which child now has the instrument. While he is guessing, everyone should be as quiet as possible. This requires good concentration on the part of the listener.

Young   Older

Let Sleeping Dogs Lie

Age group: 6–10

Requirements: a blindfold and any object

The children sit in a circle, on chairs or on the floor. One child sits on the floor in the center and is blindfolded. He is the "sleeping dog." On the ground in front of him is his "bone": a pen, a stick, or an instrument, for instance.

The leader points to another child in the circle whose task is to rob the dog of his "bone" in total silence and, of course, without the dog noticing. If the dog notices, he has to try to tag the thief, but without standing up. If he tags the thief while being robbed, the dog can stay where he is and another "thief" can try his luck. If the thief gets away with it, she becomes the next dog, and the leader picks another thief.

Which player can remain being the dog for the longest?

Older **Teens**

The Caravan

Age group: 9 and older

Requirements: instruments for all the players

The children sit in a circle with as many percussion instruments as possible and one recorder. In the game, the instruments are used to represent a caravan crossing the desert. The caravan is heard approaching slowly from far away, passing right in front of the group, and disappearing again into the distance. It should be a large caravan with camels, horses, and donkeys laden with merchandise, and lots of people. On one of the camels sits a snake charmer.

First agree on the sounds of the caravan: the people's footsteps could be played on hand drums, those of the animals on wood-blocks, the jingling of the harnesses on bells and shakers, the creaking of the packs or carts on güiros, and so on. The voices of the people can be imitated vocally, and the snake charmer's flute is the recorder, heard only when the caravan passes close by.

When all is ready, the sound collage begins: first you hear only the wind, then a cloud of dust appears on the horizon and you hear very soft, vague, low sounds. Low sounds can be heard from far away, high sounds only closer by. As the caravan approaches the sounds build up and become clearer. The leader will need to indicate clearly with her hands how close the caravan is. Only when it is close by do we hear the people's voices and the snake charmer's flute (the player should use just the high notes on the recorder). The sounds reach a peak, then the caravan goes by, and the sounds gradually become softer and softer until they fade completely and only the sound of the wind remains.

It takes a great deal of concentration on the part of the participants so that the sound flows very gradually from quiet to loud and quiet again, following the indications of the leader, and, most important, with everyone doing it together. Keep it interesting, and let the caravan move along very slowly!

Variation: For smaller children, use an image of a circus procession with horses, elephants, lions, and clowns coming down a street.

Older   Teens

Musical Typing

Age group: 10 and older

Requirements: 6 different instruments

Q	W	E	R	T		Y	U	I	O	P
1	2	3	4	5		1	2	3	4	5

XYLOPHONE   GLOCKENSPIEL

A	S	D	F	G		H	J	K	L
1	2	3	4	5		1	2	3	4

DRUM   TAMBOURINE

Z	X	C	V		V	B	N	M
1	2	3	4		4	1	2	2

WOODBLOCK   TRIANGLE

This is a typewriter or computer keyboard. Copy the table above on the blackboard, including the numbers and instruments. Explain that each letter can be played by between one and five beats on the instrument: the E is represented by three notes on the xylophone, the O by four notes on the glockenspiel, the A by one drumbeat, and so forth (use the instruments you have available).

Demonstrate how this works by playing a short sentence in "code" and asking the participants to write the message down. Now ask the participants to think of a long word, and ask a few volunteers to play their word on the instruments while the others write down the letters.

23

Older   Teens

Right-Left

Age group: 8 and older

Requirements: a drum

All the players sit on their knees in a big circle with their hands flat on the floor next to their knees. The leader plays a slow rhythm on a drum. One child begins by hitting the ground with his right hand. The child to his right does the same thing on the following beat. The child on her right does the same, and so it goes, around the circle. When one player suddenly hits the ground with two quick slaps, the player to his left has to slap the ground with her left hand on the next beat. The beat now passes to the left, and the players use their left hands. Once again someone gives two short slaps, and the beat passes to the right again. The point is to keep in rhythm with the drum. Once this is working satisfactorily with a slow rhythm, the tempo can gradually be increased.

If someone makes a mistake, by using the wrong hand or getting out of rhythm, the game stops for a moment, and that player has to continue with one hand behind her back. If she makes a second mistake, he is out.

Young

The
Triangle

Age group: 6–8

Requirements: a triangle

The children sit in a circle. The leader says, "First we're going to see if you've got good ears!" The leader takes a triangle with a metal beater, and the children close their eyes. The children have to guess how many beats are sounded on the triangle. The leader hits the triangle very slowly three or four times. Try to play the next beat just before the previous one has faded away. Then the children open their eyes, and the leader asks who heard three, four, or five beats.

Now make it harder by playing more and more softly and increasing the number of beats. The leader should stand in the center of the circle so that everyone can hear equally well. Another question: How many counts does it take for the sound of a beat on the triangle to fade away completely?

Young **Older**

Telephone Game

Age group: 7–10

Requirements: 10 sheets of paper

Ten children stand in a line facing the rest of the class. Each has a sheet of paper numbered from zero to nine. They hold the papers up so that everyone can see them. One child leaves the room. The rest of the class thinks of a well-known song, such as "Baa Baa Black Sheep." The children with the numbers are now each given a word from the song that they have to remember. Zero gets "baa," one gets the second "baa," two gets "black," and so on.

The child who left the room now comes in and "dials" his own telephone number. He calls out the numbers of his phone number one by one, and the child holding that number calls out her word. How many numbers have to be dialed before the child guesses what the song is? Then a different child leaves the room, and another song is chosen and numbered. You can, of course, also use Christmas carols or any other songs that everyone knows.

Teens

Live "Video" Game

Age group: 12 and older; 15 participants

Requirements: a large space with a playing area marked out with rope or sticky tape (see illustration); four musical instruments

In this game, two players play against each other. They each have to help a "child" to cross a busy street without being run over by a car, a bicycle, or a trolley. The traffic is represented by some players and driven by other players with instruments. There is an island in the middle of the street where the "children" can stop.

When preparing the playing area, try to keep to the distances given below. If it is much larger it will be too easy to cross the street, if it is smaller it will be too difficult. The game can be played by fifteen people, and others in the group can watch. After playing a few times, they can switch places.

The Players

1. The two main players (A and B) sit on opposite sides of the crossing. Player A has a woodblock, for instance, and player B a triangle. They use these instruments to direct the speed with which their child should cross the road.

2. Two "children" have to cross the street from opposites sides. One child follows Player A's tempo, while the other follows Player B's tempo, and both children can walk only as quickly as the tempo played by their guides. Each sound on the woodblock represents one step. The guides should play at gentle walking pace.

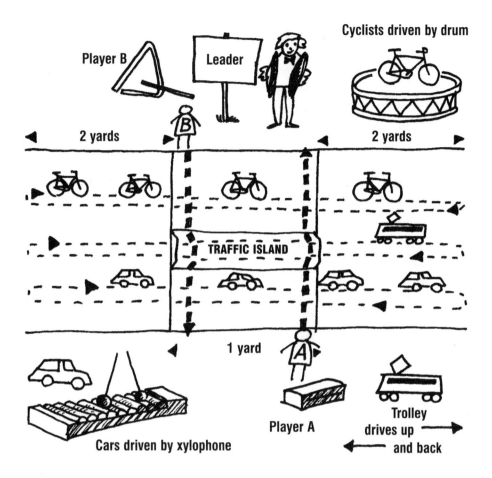

Player B

Leader

Cyclists driven by drum

2 yards

2 yards

TRAFFIC ISLAND

1 yard

Trolley
drives up →
← and back

Cars driven by xylophone

Player A

3. The cars are four children about one yard apart who walk quickly up and down the street. They move at the speed indicated by their "drivers," on a xylophone, for instance. Like robots, they react only to the sound of their own drivers. If they "crash" into one of the "children," they hold onto that her, and the leader indicates with a crash of the cymbals that the game is over.

4. The cyclists are another four children who walk slowly up and down the street about a yard apart. When they reach the end of the street they turn around and go back the other way. They are "driven" by the player with a drum, who beats it slowly to control the speed of the bicycles. Make sure that

the distance between bicycles remains about a yard. If they crash into a "child," they take hold of her and the game is over. (Crash of cymbals.)

5. Finally, down the middle of the street, including over the traffic island, runs the trolley. This is a child who moves quickly back and forth (to make the game more difficult). The guides have to watch out that if their "child" is waiting on the traffic island, he is not run over by the trolley! If he is, once again the game is over. If a player reaches the other side safely, she scores one point. Then she has to cross back over the street.

How the game works: A round is very short, so it is good to play it ten times with the same group and musicians. The winner is the "child" who has crossed the road the most times without having been run over. You can make the game more difficult by having everything move much more quickly. You may have to experiment to find the right speed. If the game is too difficult for a particular group, it can be simplified by taking away the trolley or by adding a "policeman," who can stop the traffic at will.

All Ages

Walking the Rhythm

Age group: any number of children for any age

Requirements: a piece of chalk or string

This game should be played in a large, empty room or outside.

Draw a line on the floor or lay down a rope or string. All the children should stand behind the line. The teacher stands at a considerable distance on the other side of the line and claps a very slow, short rhythm.

Now all of the children move across the line toward the teacher, taking one step—and only one step—with each clap. The teacher stops between the short rhythms to make sure that the children follow the rhythm correctly. A child who takes a step when there is no clap has to go back to the line and start again. The child that reaches the teacher first takes over the job of clapper. The clapping rhythms should be very slow at the beginning, but their speed can be increased a little as the game progresses.

Variation: The game can be made more exciting. From time to time, the teacher can unexpectedly hit a cymbal. At that sound, all the children should rush back behind the line as soon as possible. The last one to cross the line must drop out of the game.

Who will be the last child remaining?

Expression and Improvisation Games

In this category, plenty of imagination and independence are required of the players. The idea is to produce a piece of music that is largely composed by the players, using instruments, either solo or in groups.

Some games may take longer than planned, since they entail a certain amount of consultation. In the expression games the player learns to trust his own creativity and discovers that playing in a group presents more problems than simply working out the assignment. Thus this category of games brings out important aspects of learning that are also applicable to other areas of education.

First, allow the players the opportunity to discover solutions for themselves. Only if that proves impossible should you make suggestions or give an example. Stimulate their inventiveness by asking questions. Be sure to have a good selection of instruments.

Special Features

- The goal of these games is to have the players think up something for themselves. Do not expect too much from those who have had little musical experience. The most important thing may not be the result but the players' experience of being given free rein in their creativity.
- The instruments can be played to portray something in particular, for example, phenomena such as wind or rain or movements such as running or jumping. To this end, they may be played in an unusual manner (such as scratching the drumhead with the fingernails). It is helpful if you explain the possibilities to the players before they begin.

Play Like an Animal

Age group: 6–8

Requirements: 6 different instruments

Put out six instruments with different sounds (for example, a glockenspiel, a xylophone, a triangle, a woodblock, a drum, and bells). Put the names of six different animals on cards. If the children cannot read yet, make drawings of the animals. Put the names of the animals on the blackboard:

elephant — mouse — horse — lion — grasshopper — bird.

Shuffle the cards and lay them facedown in front of the instruments on the table. Let the children come up in turn, take a card, and play something on one or more instruments as that animal. The child doesn't have to imitate the sound of the animal but should be told, for instance, "play *like* a mouse," or "play *like* a horse." The child then asks the class which animal she played as. If the class guesses correctly, the next child has a turn, and the first card is placed at the bottom of the pile. If the class don't guess the animal within three tries, the child has to play again as the same animal.

After six children have had a turn, shuffle the cards and continue.

Young

Musical Conversation

Age group: 6–8

Requirements: two rhythm instruments

The children sit in a circle. Explain that they will take turns holding a conversation with another child, but using instruments instead of voices. The leader has two rhythm instruments that he sends around the circle in opposite directions. The children pass the instruments around as they sing the following song to the tune of "Frère Jacques" (write the words on the blackboard).

> **I hear talking, I hear talking**
> **On the drum, on the drum.**
> **We will see who's talking,**
> **When this song is over**
> **Bim bam bom, bim bam bom.**

The children who are holding the instruments on the final "bom" "talk" to one another: one of them plays something on the instrument, and the other answers on her own instrument. After a short conversation, the song begins again, and the instruments are passed around in the same way so that two different children can talk to each other.

Instead of singing, you can also play music while the instruments are passed around.

Older **Teens**

The Sounding Space

Age group: 10 and older

Requirements: as many instruments as possible

In this game we try to create an environment in sound so that everyone who closes their eyes and listens can immediately recognize where they are. This is done with the help of lots of different musical instruments and voices and with sounds created in the room.

On the blackboard the leader can write a list of possible locations that can be portrayed through sound and a little imagination:

- under the sea
- in the jungle or woods
- at a fair
- in a train station
- in a churchyard at night
- in a marketplace

First a volunteer is asked to leave the room. The group then picks one of the environments and tries to recreate the sounds most characteristic of that place with the help of instruments, voices, and objects in the room. They can experiment for five minutes. The sound collage need last no more than thirty seconds to one minute. Rehearse it once.

Then the volunteer is asked to come back and sit in the middle of the room with her eyes closed. In the meantime the "environment creators" have spread around the room so that the sounds come to the volunteer from every side. The listener should simply sit quiet and let the sounds wash over her, then say what the sounds remind her of. When she guesses right, the game begins again and a different scene is chosen.

Older   Teens

Musical Landscapes

Age group: 10 and older

Requirements: instruments for all the players; postcards showing landscapes

Divide the class into groups of four or five. Each participant has an instrument. Give each group a postcard of an atmospheric landscape (for example, a sunset, a snow scene, a beach with palm trees, a rushing river, and so on), or cut out suitable pictures from magazines.

For 5 or 10 minutes each group tries to recreate their landscape in sound; this should entail only atmospheric and evocative sounds, not songs. The pictures are then placed in random order on the board, after which each group in turn plays their landscape without saying which one it is. The rest of the group guesses which landscape is being played.

Young

Find Your Own Instrument

Age group: 6–9

Requirements: cards with the names of instruments; a recording of restful music

Each child is given a card with the name of an instrument on it (for example, violin, piano, cello, flute, harp, and so on). Each instrument is named on two cards.

Some restful music is played, and the participants walk around in time to the music, miming playing their instrument. As they do so, they look around to see who else is playing the same instrument, and they pair up with that person.

When everyone has found their partner, the music stops and the leader calls out the name of one of the instruments, for example, piano. The two "pianists" come forward and face the group. We now have a concerto for piano and orchestra: the two pianists are the soloists and the rest of the group the orchestra. The orchestra sings a well-known song, and the pianists mime the piano part. When the song is finished, two other soloists are chosen, and the orchestra sings another song.

Don't forget to applaud the soloists!

Older   Teens

What Am I Playing?

Age group: 8 and older

Requirements: 6 different instruments

Six different instruments are placed in front of the class. Each instrument is given a number between one and six, so that the players can choose an instrument by rolling a die. The instruments are then written on the board in the following manner:

•	drum (or bongo)
• •	tambourine (or shaker)
• • •	glockenspiel (or metallophone)
• • • •	xylophone (or recorder)
• • • • •	triangle (or bells)
• • • • • •	woodblock (or bongo drums)

One child begins by throwing a die: the number of points indicates the instrument he is to play. With this instrument he portrays something, and the rest of the class has to guess what it is. He does not play a tune, but imitates something. A drum, for instance, could be played to imitate the sound of footsteps or thunder, a tambourine could be played to sound like a sleigh or the jingle of coins, a glockenspiel could be the sound of a doorbell or a babbling brook, and bongo drums or a woodblock could be a galloping horse. Anyone with an idea can come up, throw the die, pick up the instrument and play something.

If the class can't guess the right answer right away, the sound is repeated. If it is not guessed by the third try, someone else has a turn.

Young

The Playground Game

Age group: 6–9

Requirements: an instrument for each child; copies of the drawings below

Divide the class into four groups. Give each group a drawing of an object in the playground:

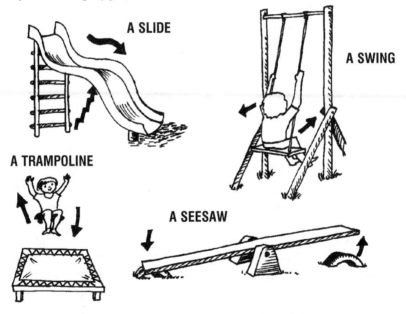

A SLIDE

A SWING

A TRAMPOLINE

A SEESAW

Each group now prepares to depict in sound the activity relating to their particular drawing (with the help of glockenspiel, xylophones, drums, and various rhythm instruments). If necessary certain sounds (sliding sounds, for example) can be made with the voice. After a few minutes each group performs what they have prepared, while the rest of the class has to guess what is being depicted.

Older

35

Sound Riddle

Age group: 8–10

Divide the class into groups of four or five. Each group chooses an event, a situation, or a short story that they will explain in sound alone. The sounds can only be made with the voice or hands: whistling, buzzing, singing, laughing, crying, hissing, clapping, and so forth. No words or pantomime are allowed.

After about ten minutes of preparation time, during which the groups do not know what the others are doing, each group presents their "play" in turn and the others guess what they are doing.

Older   **Teens**

36

Speaking or Shouting

Age group: 10 and older

Requirements: several melody and rhythm instruments

A table is placed at the front of the class with an assortment of melody and rhythm instruments on each side. The children come up in twos and stand on either side of the table. They each choose an instrument with which to speak to their partner.

One begins, the other answers. This can go one of two ways: it can be a pleasant conversation lasting one minute, or it can turn into an argument with shouting and yelling (on the instruments). Which will it be? It should last no longer than a minute but can be shorter.

Older   Teens

The Dice
Game

Age group: 10 and older

Requirements: a die, which is homemade

For each face of the die think of a sound and suitable rhythm. This can be prepared in advance by the leader or agreed on by the participants during the class. For example:

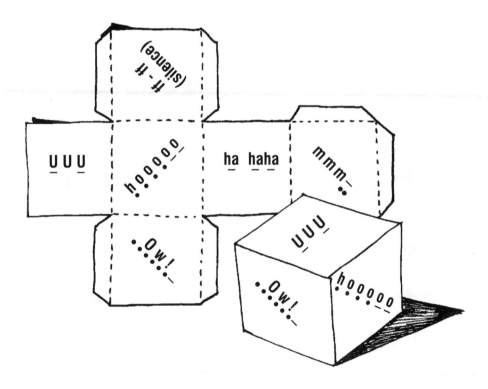

1. (sound)   U U U
   (rhythm)   –   –
   (in 4/4 time)

2. (sound)   h o o o o o
   (rhythm)   • • • • – –

3. (sound)   ha haha
   (rhythm)   – – –

4. (sound)   m m m –
   (rhythm)   ••

5. (sound)   ff-ff
   (rhythm)   (silence)

6. (sound)   Ow!
   (rhythm)   • • • • •–

• = short note, – = long note

The series of sounds can be written on the board or on a large die made of cardboard. Divide the class into six groups. The sounds are made with the voice and the rhythm with hand clapping. First practice all the sounds so that they can be made simultaneously in a gentle four-beat rhythm.

The groups take turns throwing the die. At a signal from the leader the group begins playing the sound corresponding to the number on the die. They continue to play as the next group throw the die and join in and so on, until everyone is playing. If a number that is already being played is thrown, that group stops playing until their number is thrown again. The game stops at a signal from the leader. The finish can either be a sudden end or a gradual fading into silence.

38

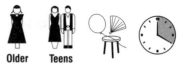

Older   Teens

Dancing Hands

Age group: 10 and older

Requirements: drawing paper and pencils for each participant; classical dance music

Each participant has a sheet of paper and a pencil. Put on a piece
of lively classical dance music such as a Strauss waltz, one of
Brahms's *Hungarian Dances,* or the *Sabre Dance* by Khatchaturian
—or any suitable dance music you have in your collection. Ask the
class to perform a dance or ballet to the music—but using only a
pencil. They can draw sweeping lines and pirouettes on the paper
in time to the music. Now ask them to fill in the lines with colors.
They can create some very beautiful abstract drawings in this
manner.

Young   Older

Train Game

Age group: 6–10

You are riding on the train and looking out of the window. What can you see outside that reminds you of a song? You might see hills or a church (which might make you think of "Jack and Jill" or "Oranges and Lemons"). The train could also go through forests ("The Ash Grove") or places where you might see animals ("The Animals Went in Two by Two").

Someone in the class with an idea that appears in a song comes up and draws it on the board. As soon as someone else guesses which song it is, she sings the song. She then comes up to the board and makes a drawing of her own. If she can't think of anything, she can pass the chalk to someone else.

Music: That's What You Are

Age group: 12 and older

The participants stand in a circle, and the leader asks them all to think of a sound that suits them. For instance, someone who is very rhythmic makes up a short rhythm that he can play using body sounds or his voice; someone who is more melodic thinks up a short melody of a few notes; any other type of sound can be made, as long as it suits the person making it. The players should find their sound inside themselves first and not immediately make it out loud.

One volunteer goes to the center of the circle. She is the conductor. She waves her hands and points at someone, and this person now makes his sound. The conductor then points to others, who all make their sounds when signaled to do so. Then the conductor can point to two or three people at the same time and create an entire composition.

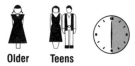

Older   Teens

Musical Mandala

Age group: 10 and older

A mandala is usually a round, symmetrical drawing with a symbolic meaning. The musical counterpart is a "mantra": a religious phrase that is sung over and over to a simple melody. You can make up your own mantra by setting a well-known saying to a very simple melody. It should be a melody using just a few notes that can easily be repeated.

Divide the group into pairs. Write about ten short sayings on the board, and let each pair choose one and make up a melody that is easy to repeat.

Some suitable sayings are:

Every cloud has a silver lining.

A rolling stone gathers no moss.

East, west, home is best.

While the cat's away the mice will play.

The early bird catches the worm.

Make hay while the sun shines.

After five or ten minutes of preparation, let each couple sing their "mantra," after which the whole class can join in with them. Which one was the class favorite? Sing that one again with an instrumental accompaniment.

Older   **Teens**

The Skating Felt Pen

Age group: 10 and older

Requirements: drawing paper and felt pens for each child

Each child has a sheet of paper and a felt pen. First, the players draw a big lake. In the lake they draw a couple of small circles. The lake is frozen, and the circles are the holes in the ice where the ducks are swimming. The leader puts on some romantic dance or ballet music often used with figure skating, such as a waltz by Tchaikovsky or Strauss. The felt pen is now a skater who glides and sweeps over the ice. Let the pen make the same kind of movements that you would make on the ice, making curlicues and circles around the holes.

Variation: Two children with different colored pens "skate" together on the same piece of paper.

Young

Musical Fish

Age group: 6–8

Requirements: 20–30 cardboard fish with paperclips; a fishing rod with a magnet at the end of the line

Make 20–30 cardboard fish (see example) and write a musical task on the back of each. There must be three types of tasks: simple, medium, and difficult. The fish with the easy tasks are marked with a one on the front, the medium ones with a two, and the difficult ones with a three. There should be at least as many fish as there are children. Fix a paperclip to each fish and put all of the fish in a large box. Make a fishing rod out of a stick and a piece of string with a magnet on the end.

Let the children take turns catching a fish and performing the task written on it. If they do this well, they can keep the fish. If they can't do it, they throw the fish back and try another. If a player still can't do it, let another child have a turn catching fish. Who has the most points when everyone has had a turn?

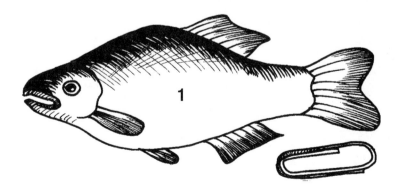

Tasks (think of more yourself):

Simple (one point):
- imitate a bee
- click three times with your tongue
- dance once around a chair
- imitate the sound a fish makes
- whistle like a canary
- sing from high to low

Medium (two points):
- clap "Baa Baa Black Sheep" with your hands
- sing your highest note
- sing your lowest note
- imitate a bird on an instrument
- draw a musical instrument
- march up and down like a soldier

Difficult (three points):
- snap a rhythm with your fingers
- play "Mary Had a Little Lamb" on a glockenspiel (begin on E)
- play "Three Blind Mice" on a sound stave
- sing a song of your choice
- play a march on a drum
- dance around the table on one leg

Rhythm Games

The games in this section can be seen as part of elementary musical education. If they are repeated fairly frequently they will increase the players' skills of clapping or playing many different rhythms.

The first four games in particular are designed for beginners; they aim to teach, in a light-hearted way, very simple rhythms, including how to play them in time. The same games can also be played later with instruments. The rest of the games assume that the children are familiar with simple rhythms and offer the opportunity to think up their own rhythms or improvise. In this sense they are both expression and improvisation games, but within a strict rhythmic framework.

Before rhythm instruments are used, the children should be given instructions about the right way to play them. If they have no skills in playing rhythm instruments, nothing much will come of rhythmic improvisations.

Special Features

- The simplest games are intended to train the children how to play in time with the help of simple rhythms.
- The more difficult rhythm games are intended to give practice and skill in the use of various rhythm instruments.
- These games contribute to the children's rhythmic education and can be used as such during the course of music lessons.

44

Young

Word Clapping Game

Age group: 5–6

This is a simple rhythm game for children who can't read yet. Make four drawings on the board representing words with one, two, three, and four syllables respectively: tree, spider, elephant, and alligator.

Each child in turn claps the rhythm of one of the drawings. The class has to guess which word it is. Longer words, such as "hippopotamus" or "video camera" can also be used.

Young

Name Game

Age group: 6–8

Requirements: a hand drum

This is also a good game for children to use to get to know each other. The children sit in a circle. The leader plays a gentle 4/4 rhythm on a drum, and the children clap in time. One by one, the children call out their first and last name in a rhythm of their choice, though it must fit with the 4/4 rhythm being played. If necessary the leader can help. Some names can be spoken in several different rhythms. The players continue chanting their names in the 4/4 rhythm played by the leader, and each time one more name is added. When everyone is chanting together, the leader starts pointing to the children in turn, and they stop one by one until only the drum remains.

At the end of the game the players will certainly know one another's names!

Young

Start and Stop

Age group: 6–8

Write the following rhythm on the board:

da - da   da - da   dom   dom   dom   da - da dom   dom

Read it out rhythmically and ask the children to join in. Repeat the rhythm several times. Think of a signal to use to get them to stop. Ask the players to repeat the rhythm again several times, and test them to see if your stop signal works. Continue until everyone reacts correctly. Then think up a starting signal, upon which the whole class starts the rhythm at the same time. Practice the start and stop signals a few times until everyone reacts perfectly. Then let one child come to the front to give the start and stop signals.

Next divide the class into two and ask the second group to begin one beat later than the first group. Give each group its own start and stop signals so that the two groups chant sometimes solo, sometimes in unison and sometimes in parts.

Young

Before and After

Age group: 6–8

Have the children sing,

> One — two — three-four-five,
> Once I caught a fish a-live
> Six — seven — eight-nine-ten,
> Then I let him go a-gain
>
> Why — did you let him go?
> Because he bit my finger so
> Which — finger did he bite?
> The little one upon the right.

and then just clap the rhythm. Next speak the words rhythmically: the teacher says the first line (one, two, three…) and the children answer with the second line (once I caught a fish alive), and so on. Then do it the other way around: the class begins and the teacher answers. Use the start and stop signals from the previous game. Have two groups start one beat after the other so that the rhythm becomes a canon.

Now think of signals for loud and soft, and use them in combination with the start and stop signals.

Young

Fast or Slow

Age group: 6–8

Requirements: a large drum and a hand drum or tambourine

The children sit in a circle. Teach them to chant the following rhyme rhythmically and in time:

<u>Fast</u> or <u>slow</u>
<u>any</u> way you <u>go</u>
<u>your</u> turn's <u>coming</u>
<u>now</u>!

The leader plays a slow 2/4 rhythm on a large drum or timpani. The children pass a hand drum or tambourine around the circle in time with the drumbeat. While they do so, they chant the verse above, also in time with the drum.

On the word "now" they stop chanting, and the child holding the instrument plays a fast or slow rhythm solo, if possible, also in time with the big drum. When she has done this, she passes the hand drum on, and all the players begin chanting again.

49

Young

Drumming

Age group: 6–9 years

Requirements: 12 drums

Six children each get a drum and sit in a line facing six other children who also each have a drum.

The first child starts by hitting her drum once. The child facing her imitates this exactly. The second child beats his drum twice, and the child facing him repeats this rhythm. The third child hits her drum three times, the fourth hits his drum four times, and this is continued until the sixth child is reached. Then the opposite row starts.

The children in the first line can play their number of beats in any rhythm they want, and the children in the second line should try to imitate their rhythms exactly. After a few turns, the teacher can play a slow, basic beat on a large drum or clap, and the children should try to keep their rhythm within this basic beat. The teacher can also give some examples of the different rhythms that can be played using one to six beats.

Variation: Draw one to six dots in squares on the blackboard, just like on a die. The teacher then points at random to one of the squares and the children take turns playing that number of beats in a rhythm of their own choice on their own drums.

Once the children are familiar with playing the rhythms, one of the children can be the "conductor" instead of the teacher.

Find Your Own Rhythm

Age group: 10–12

Requirements: four rhythm instruments

This game is played by eight people at the same time, but because it is quite short, everyone in the class will get their turns quickly. Four children take a drum or other rhythm instrument. The leader gives each instrument a short rhythm phrase of its own.

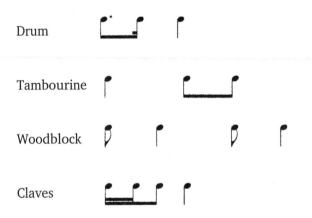

Drum

Tambourine

Woodblock

Claves

Practice until everyone has his own rhythm memorized. Choose four other children and assign each of them one of the rhythms—so the drum rhythm belongs to child one, the tambourine rhythm belongs to child two, and so on. Make sure that the four children recognize their rhythms. Put the four players with the instruments at least one yard apart on one side of an empty room. The four other children are blindfolded and stand on the opposite side of the room. The rhythm players now play their rhythms one by one in random order. When a blindfolded child hears "his" rhythm, he takes one step forward. This is repeated until all the blindfolded children have reached their own rhythm player. Then play the same game with eight other children.

You can make the game harder by having the rhythm players silently change places now and then. The leader should ensure that the blindfolded children don't bump into anything that could hurt them.

Young

Guessing Game

Age group: 6–8

Requirements: 1 hand drum

Write the titles of ten well-known children's songs on the board. You can also use any popular songs, as long as everyone knows them. One child starts by playing the rhythm of one of the songs on a hand drum. As soon as someone guesses which song it is, she takes a turn.

Teens

The Secret Rhythm

Age group: 12–16

Write four short messages on the board, all of which can be played rhythmically and are all quite distinct from one another.

1. At nine o' clock to - night...

2. An - y - one want to car - ry this?

3. Wear yel - low rib - bons.

4. Eve-ry-one must be in - side by ten thir - ty.

First teach the class to clap these four rhythms. Then divide the players into four groups. The groups stand in line, one behind the other, so that everyone is facing the back of the person in front. You now have four rows of people facing the board so that they can read the sentences.

The teacher now taps out one of the messages on the back of the child at the back of one row—a different message for each row, of course. The children at the back of each row tap the same rhythm on the back of the person in front, who does the same to the person in front of him. When it reaches the child at the front, she tells the leader which message she received. The first child to say the message correctly can give out the rhythms for the next round.

Young   Older

Rhythmic Orchestra Game

Age group: 6–10

Requirements: instruments for each player

Divide the class into four groups. Each group has the same type of rhythm instruments. For instance, group A has drums, group B has tambourines and maracas, group C has xylophones and glockenspiels, and group D has castanets and woodblocks. Now you have an orchestra made up of four groups.

Choose a well-known song (like "Sing a Song of Sixpence") and ask each group in turn to play one line rhythmically on their instruments. So group A plays just "Sing a song of sixpence," group B plays "a pocket full of rye," and so on.

Have one child come to the front of the class and conduct by pointing to the group that has to play their line. When this is done, ask another child to pick a new song and start again.

Older   Teens

Call and Response

Age group: 8 and older

Requirements: various hand drums

This game is based on call-and-response, an element that is very common in African and East Indian music: a soloist plays or sings a line or phrase, and the group echoes it back. All the children have a drum or clap with their hands. The teacher or one of the pupils beats time on a big drum, for example, one beat on a slow count of four. The children come up one by one, stand in front of the class, and play on a drum a simple rhythm that fits between two beats of the big drum—that is, a 4/4 rhythm. The class then imitates or "responds" to them. The soloist should preferably begin on the first beat with the class following on the next beat. Then the soloist plays a different pattern and the class imitates. Try to keep in time.

After a few calls and responses, a new soloist comes to the front. The soloists should try to play different rhythms, but if some of the children find this too difficult they can repeat the same rhythm a few times.

Older

Song Rhythm Game

Age group: 8–12

Requirements: a die and a drum (optional)

First write two well-known songs on the board, with the words divided over six lines. Mark them A and B:

A. "My Bonnie Lies over the Ocean"
1. My bonnie lies over the ocean
2. My bonnie lies over the sea
3. My bonnie lies over the ocean
4. Oh, bring back my bonnie to me
5. Bring back, oh bring back, bring back my bonnie to me, to me
6. Bring back, oh bring back, bring back my bonnie to me

B. "Clementine"
1. In a cavern, in a canyon
2. Excavating for a mine
3. Lived a miner, forty-niner
4. And his daughter, Clementine
5. Oh my darling, oh my darling, oh my darling Clementine
6. Thou art lost and gone forever, dreadful sorry Clementine

Whatever song you choose it must be divided into six lines and numbered (if using a song with eight lines, put two lines together).

Two children play opposite each other; they have to clap or drum the rhythm of each line correctly. One plays song A, the other plays song B: this is decided by chance. They roll the die, and the number indicates which line the child has to clap or drum. If she does it right (in the leader's judgment—and it can be played once only) the leader marks that line on the board, and the child can throw again. If, in the leader's judgment, the rhythm was not correct, the other child starts with his song (and, of course, the line from the first song is not marked off). If a number is thrown a second time, the other child has a turn. When one child gets all six lines marked off, it is the turn of two other children.

After using these songs a few times, choose two new ones. For older children you could ask them to find songs that have six lines ("When the Saints Go Marching In," "Mi Caballo Blanco")—especially non-English-language songs—and teach them to the rest of the class.

Sound Games

These sound games are a specific type of expression game. They each use a drawing as the basis for a musical sound collage.

This kind of game is like playing music from a normal score, but it is more lighthearted, and the scope for interpretations is somewhat wider. It is a musical activity in which anyone can take part, regardless of his or her level of musical skill. Through play the pupils become familiar with alternative forms of musical notation and with another idiom of sound. These games, therefore, are also an important ingredient in musical education. By playing these games the pupils learn about the most important musical parameters such as pitch, time, sound color, the use of the voice, and instrumentation.

Special Features

- Through these games the students can discover that they can use their voices and instruments in countless different ways to produce a musical result.
- The students familiarize themselves with written musical scores in a playful manner.

Young **Older**

The Tree of Sound

Age group: 6–12

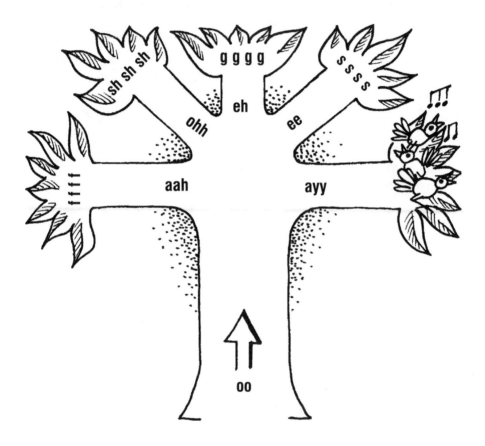

Sound drawings, such as the "tree of sound" above, are an enjoyable way of giving children a basic concept of graphic notation. The tree, which should be copied on the blackboard, is purely for vocalization. The teacher uses a stick to point to the trunk of the tree, where it says "oo." The children then sing out a low "oo" sound. Agree in advance that they should continue to sing the sound as long as the stick is resting on that sound. Moving the stick upward indicates that the note gets higher, moving it down, lower. Moving to the left or right indicates that the note remains the same, but the sound itself changes.

Once that concept is clear we take another look at the tree: the trunk consists of a strong "oo" sound that starts low and gets steadily higher; the branches are vowels that are sung at the same pitch or rise to a greater or lesser degree. The leaves are consonants that are sounded as long as they are pointed to, while the leaves on the right have only the sound of bird song.

The tree can be used in different ways: the teacher begins at the foot of the trunk and goes slowly to the first branch on the left: the "oo" sound changes into an "aah" sound and finishes with a sustained "fffff." Then the teacher takes the stick off the board, so there is a moment's silence, and begins from the base of the trunk again and goes up to another branch. You can also go from the leaves back down the branch and over to another branch, so that the whole tree can be "sung" without a break. After a few tries, ask one of the children to "conduct" the class through the tree. Of course, you can fill in other sounds and letters. The tree can also be drawn by the children.

Young   Older

Dead-End Street

Age group: 6–12

The dead-end street is based on the same principles as the tree of sound, except that here we use rougher and more aggressive sounds characteristic of traffic.

The idea is to imitate a car with a droning "aaah" sound. The car enters a series of one-way streets (whereupon the sound changes) and crashes into a wall. The sounds of the crash vary according to street. Here again, you can go back to the start over and over again, or turn the car around after a crash and continue. Let the children conduct as well.

Young   Older

The Racetrack

Age group: 6–12 years

In this sound game the class can be divided into two groups. One group represents the racing car, the other the spectators. This game is also played entirely with the voice.

After a loud "bang" from the starting pistol, the car starts with a "vroom" sound from the engine. This quickly rises and changes into a squeaking "eee" sound from the tires at the bend. As the car goes past the spectators (the other group), they cheer and shout, until after the second bend, when the car flies out of control with an enormous "wham" and, with lots of crashing and squealing, rolls over and lands on its roof. Then there is a moment's silence until we hear the siren of the ambulance...The end.

A Sound Walk Through Nature

Age group: 10–16

Requirements: instruments for all the players

This sound drawing is performed with instruments. You should provide as many different types of instruments as possible. The idea is to depict a walk by using sound; you can use the drawing to suggest the sounds heard on the walk. The illustration (or your own variation) should be drawn on the board. Talk with the students about the types of sounds a person might hear while walking from the woods on the left to the seashore on the right, and how these sounds can be represented on the instruments.

First come the woodland sounds: How do you make the sound of the wind in the trees, the singing of the birds? Try it out! Then comes a village where the church clock is striking the hour. What time is it? It starts to rain, first just a few drops, then more and more, harder and harder. How can you imitate that sound? Then comes a storm with thunder and lightning! Let the thunder be loud; the storm clouds will blow over quickly. Storm and rain sounds fade gradually until our wanderers reach the beach, where we can hear the sea, the sounds of the surf, and the wind. From the distance comes the sound of a ship's foghorn...

Of course, the walker's footsteps will be heard the whole time: they can be played by one student on a hand drum. It is a good idea (and will increase the concentration level) if you record the sounds of this walk and listen to them again in a later class.

Older   Teens

A Sound Walk
Through the House

Age group: 10–16

Requirements: instruments for all the players

If you feel it will take too long to copy the illustration on the board, you can also represent the sounds in the various different spaces in a house without a drawing. In that case, draw a simple plan and write in the names of the rooms:

- living room
- kitchen
- bathroom
- bedroom

Ask the students to call out the most common sounds associated with each room and write them on the board. This will result in a list something like this:

- living room: conversation/children playing/TV or radio sounds
- kitchen: rattling of pots and pans/whistling of kettle
- bathroom: running water/someone singing in the shower/flushing the toilet
- bedroom: snoring/alarm clock

First agree on whether the entire class will make the sounds for all the rooms or if smaller groups will take one room each. Then practice and find the right instruments for making the sounds as realistic as possible. When everything is clearly worked out, agree on a route through the house and create a four-part sound collage.

This collage can also be recorded and played back during a later session.

Older

Body Music

Age group: 8–12

This is a sound game using the sounds of our own bodies. What can we do with our hands? Clap, rub, or snap the fingers. What can we do with our feet? Stamp or shuffle. What can we do with the mouth? Whistle, hiss, click with the tongue, or make other noises. We can write these three types of sounds as a simple score using symbols to represent the sounds.

Explain the following symbols to the class:

> **c = hand clapping**
> **s = snapping the fingers**
> **r = rubbing the fingers together**
> **f = stamping the feet**
> **sh = shuffling the feet**
> **+ = clicking the tongue**

Other vocal sounds can be spelled out.

Here is an example of a sound score:

Hands:	s s s s	s r r	c c c c	c c c c
Feet:		f f	sh sh	
Mouth:			+ "wow"	"fa fa fa fa"

This series of sounds can be repeated twice. There is, of course, no rhythm, but when the teacher points to the symbols at a leisurely tempo one after the other, the whole class can make the sounds at the same time. Then ask one of the children to write a score of her own and conduct it.

Variation: If you substitute dots and dashes for the letters, you can give the players a playful introduction to the concepts of "musical score" and "sound collage."

Older   Teens

The Voyage to Treasure Island

Age group: 10 and older

Requirements: instruments for all the players

The illustration shows a ship's passage from its departure from the harbor on a long voyage to an unknown island where there is said to be treasure. The sailors discover the treasure and, after a voyage beset with danger, return home again. The illustration should be copied on the board or photocopied and enlarged and hung in front of the class.

The game is, of course, about depicting the sounds in the drawing, but you can lend it a greater degree of musical unity by giving the "ship" a theme, say a four-note motif that is repeated throughout. This could be played on a vibraphone or piano. This motif can be composed by the pupils themselves and played by one or two in unison.

Divide the class into four groups:

1. the ship (one or two children with instruments)
2. sea sounds (sounds of the waves, foghorns, and so on)
3. whales and seagulls (these can be done vocally)
4. other sounds (drumming of the islanders, jingling of treasure)

These sounds should be rehearsed beforehand. Once they have been practiced enough, the journey can begin. Follow the dotted line on the drawing.

a) The ship leaves, the anchor chain rattles, a foghorn sounds.
b) The ship's theme plays and continues throughout the game, except when it is on the island.
c) The sounds of surf and waves continue as long as they are at sea (but they should not drown out the ship's theme).
d) The "sailors" hear whales (long, resounding "oo" sounds with the voice; listen to a recording of whale song).

e) They reach the shore of the island and walk to where the treasure is buried (ship and sea themes stop, footsteps); in the distance they hear the islanders drumming.

f) They find the treasure (cries of joy; delighted jingling of the gold pieces).

e) They return to the ship (footsteps) and set sail for home (ship and sea sounds).

g) They blow off course and run into a heavy storm.

h) Gradually the storm passes and they hear whales again.

i) Still later they hear the cries of seagulls and know that land is not far off, and finally they arrive home safely (everything becomes quiet).

(Based on an idea by Christopher Denman in *Music in the Making: Ten Scenarios*. Reprinted with the permission of Cambridge University Press.)

Teens

The Pinball Machine

Age group: 12–16

Requirements: at least 8 different instruments

The group has the eight instruments shown in the drawing on the next page: cymbals, drum, shaker or bells, tambourine, glockenspiel, vibraphone, maracas, and woodblock. Each instrument can also be played by two people so that sixteen rather than eight players can take part at the same time.

Copy the pinball machine illustration on the blackboard, or make your own version. The leader uses a stick to point out where the ball is rolling. The ball can go in by one of two entrances and, after bouncing back and forth reaches "game over." The idea is for the children to play their instruments at the moment the ball touches them, as indicated by the teacher's pointer. When the teacher points to the start, the firing of the ball is signified by a clash of cymbals. The ball can then bounce off the woodblock and between the glockenspiels (descending glissando!), bump up against the tambourine, and be flipped upward again (drumbeat), and so on.

After the teacher has demonstrated once or twice, members of the class can take turns playing pinball. If the flippers react too late with their drumbeat when the ball comes, it rolls between them to "game over."

A Musical Pinball Machine

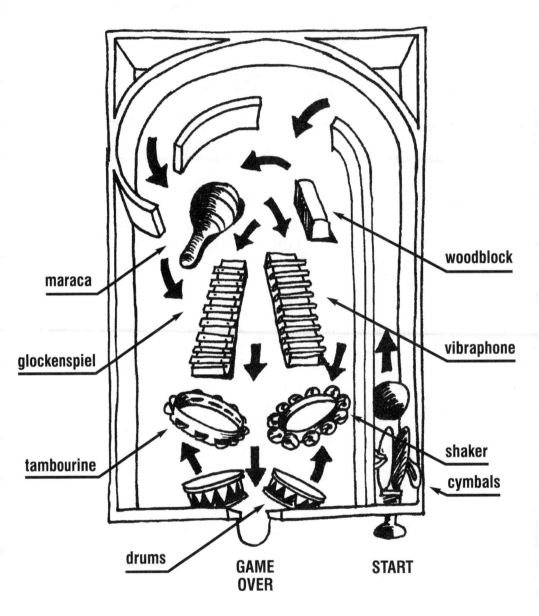

maraca

woodblock

glockenspiel

vibraphone

tambourine

shaker

cymbals

drums

GAME
OVER

START

Teens

Making and Guessing Graphical Scores

Age group: 12 and older

Requirements: instruments for half the group

First explain what a musical score is: using dots and dashes you can give a general idea of the sounds of voices and instruments. Demonstrate this on the board with vocal sounds. Then ask the children to form pairs and write down a simple musical score for one voice and one instrument. Each pair has one instrument: one plays and the other makes vocal sounds.

When the score is ready (after ten minutes or so) each score is given a number; write the number in large figures in the top or bottom corner so that everyone can see it. The scores themselves should also be written large. The scores are then hung or laid out in such a way that the whole class can read them. Since there are only numbers and no names, no one except the composers themselves knows who has written which score.

Then ask the groups to perform their own composition without saying which score they are reading (they are in no particular order). Everyone else has to guess which score is being played, and write down the number. After each performance the teacher can give the composition's number and ask who guessed correctly.

Here is an example of a graphical score for one voice and instrument (see games 37 and 61).

```
    • = short note       —— = long note

voice:      ooh ooh la la   lu          lu lu ah ah  ooh
              •   •   •  •    ——          •  •  •  •   ——
instrument:  ——                  •  •  •  •    ——  •  •  ——
```

All Ages

The Weather Game

Age group: all ages

Requirements: as many instruments as possible

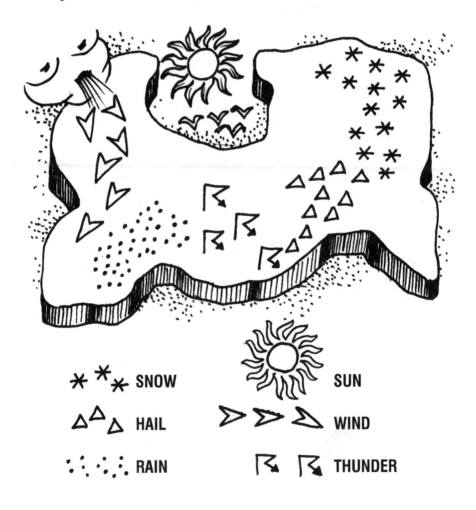

✳✳✳ **SNOW**

△△△ **HAIL**

∴∴∴ **RAIN**

SUN

⟩⟩⟩ **WIND**

THUNDER

Draw an imaginary island on the board with six different types of weather. In Fantasyland all types of weather prevail at the same time: in one place the sun is shining, in other places it is raining, hailing, or snowing. Be sure to provide a key to the symbols so that everyone understands what they mean.

Divide the instruments among the players and begin by trying out how they can portray all different kinds of weather. For example, the sun and birds can be made with cheerful sounds on the glockenspiel and whistled or played on a flute; rain with tapping or drumming the fingers on drums and tables; the wind with wind instruments and "whooo" sounds; thunder with loud drumbeats and cymbals; hail with fast tapping on wood instruments; snow with very soft, dampened sounds with the fingers on xylophones, glockenspiels, and so forth.

Now use a pointer to trace a journey through Fantasyland where the participants play the different weather types. Then let a few of the group members fill in their own weather types and lead the journey.

Dance and Movement Games

These dance and movement games fall under the category of creative dancing. They are not existing folk or jazz dances; to a greater or lesser extent the participants themselves improvise the dances within a given framework. As such they form a good follow-up to *101 Dance Games for Children* by Paul Rooyackers.

For these dance games a large empty space or gym, with a sound system or CD player, is recommended. The choice of music is, in general, reasonably open. With each game there is a recommendation as to style; this recommendation is very general, for example, it might be for fast dance music, disco, or a slow waltz. Leaders can then choose suitable music from their own collections.

A number of games are based on recognizing simple musical structures and as such contribute to elementary music and dance education.

Special Features

- Dance and movement games help the students to improvise and enhance their feel for time and rhythm.
- They are particularly suitable for closing a lesson or period to burn off excess energy.
- The "enchanted disco," the "car dance," and "the limbo" are ideal dances for self-expression.

Young   Older

The Standing Dance

Age group: 6–10

Requirements: disco or other rhythmic music

The players stand in a circle or spread around the room. The leader explains that in the beginning they must stay perfectly still and not move a muscle. Then he will "liberate" the body parts one by one: when he calls out the name of a body part they can move that part in time to the music, and not before. Once its name is called out, that part can stay in motion while other parts are added.

The leader puts on some strongly rhythmic music (like disco) and after a few moments calls out "little finger, right hand." Everyone starts moving just that finger. Next she might say the head, left thumb, right foot, left shoulder, mouth, right hand, left leg, hips, and so on, until the entire body is moving. The players all remain standing in one place.

After this the body can be "closed down" again, by calling out the names of the parts to stop moving, until everyone is once again standing completely still and the dance is over.

Young   Older

Stick
Dance

Age group: 6–10

Requirements: slow waltz music; sticks or newspapers

The children make themselves two sticks out of rolled-up newspapers, or they can use wooden sticks about a foot long. The sticks can also be decorated with ribbons.

The players form pairs and kneel on the floor facing each other. Each pair thinks of three different movements they can make with the sticks on three beats of a 3/4 rhythm. Both partners make the movements at the same time, in a mirror image. The leader puts on a slow waltz and beats time so that all the children keep to the beat:

> First beat: sticks tap the ground
> Second beat: cross your sticks over
> Third beat: cross your sticks with your partner's

Young

Dance to
the Sign

Age group: 6–9

Requirements: recordings of different kinds of dance music

Have every child choose a partner. Have each child face his partner at a distance of about three feet. One child of each pair has the task of conducting the other's movements using hand signs. For instance, if the "conductor" moves his hand up and down, the dancer hops up and down. If the conductor moves his hand to the right, the dancer takes a few steps to the right, etc. After a few minutes, the conductor and the dancer switch roles.

At first, have the children attempt the activity without music. When everybody understands the signs, let them dance to slow music. Play faster music as the children get more comfortable with the signs.

Variation: Select one child as the "dance teacher" and have the others stand at a distance facing her. Have the entire group dance to the signs of the dance teacher. Choose another child as the dance teacher after a few minutes and play different music.

Older   Teens

The Car Dance

Age group: 10 and older

Requirements: boogie-woogie or rhythm and blues music

This dance consists of six different "steps" representing the movements made when we drive a car. Each step consists of four counts that are repeated, first four counts right, then four counts left, so that the whole dance consists of twelve bars of four beats. The best music to use is the blues, since it consists of cycles of twelve bars: this dance can also be called a "blues dance." Or you may find boogie-woogie the most suitable music for this game. With this type of music it is easy to hear when the twelve-bar cycle begins again, so you can clearly hear when to start the series of steps again.

Divide the group into two and have them stand in rows about two yards apart, facing each other. To begin, it is best to write the series of "steps" on the blackboard:

1. accelerate (push the right foot forwards four times as if pressing the accelerator pedal; repeat with the left foot)

2. open windows (make small circles with the right hand as if winding down the window; repeat with the left hand)

3. steer (make a circular movement with both hands as if holding the steering wheel; first four turns to the right, then four turns to the left)

4. do windshield wipers (move your hands back and forth crossing over in front of your face)

5. change gear (move the right hand back and forth four times as if moving the gear lever; repeat with the left hand)

6. open the sunroof (make a circular movement above the head with the right hand; repeat with the left hand)

Then the series begins again—this is exactly two bars. Continue repeating the series until the music finishes. It goes without saying that, along with the hand and foot movements, the body should also sway in time to the music and the arm movements can be exaggerated.

Teens

The Enchanted Disco

Age group: 12 and older

Requirements: disco music with a slow introduction

In this game everyone travels to an enchanted disco on another planet, where the strangest things can happen. Begin by forming a large circle with everyone facing outward in a squatting position with arms linked. First we go by spaceship to another planet. Choose a piece of lively dance music (like disco) with a slow introduction.

During the introduction the dancers slowly rise up (the start), and at the moment the rhythm begins they let go of one another's arms and with a leap, turn to face the center of the circle (the landing), and start a freestyle dance to the music. Suddenly the leader turns the music down and calls out, "We're standing on a volcano and the ground is getting hotter and hotter!" Then the dancers go on as if the ground is hot, and the music continues.

The music stops again, and the leader says, "The ceiling is caving in!" The dancers continue bent over. Then the room starts shrinking; the dancers come closer and closer together. Then there is a meteorite storm, and, last, the gravity in the room increases. The dancers get heavier and heavier until they are pushed flat on the floor and can't move at all, at which point the dance is over!

Older   Teens

In Rhythm, Out of Rhythm

Age group: 10 and older

At a signal from the leader, everyone walks around the room in their own tempo. There is no music. At a second signal everyone tries to walk in the same tempo until you can hear a clear walking rhythm. Is it fast or slow? How long does it take? Then once again they walk at their own pace until the next signal: everyone in time, and so on.

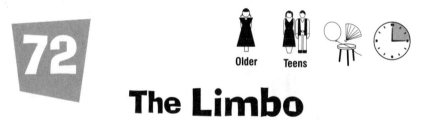

Older   Teens

The Limbo

Age group: 10 and older

Requirements: Caribbean dance music; a broomstick or pole

All the children dance freely in a circle to the sound of lively Caribbean (for example, calypso) music. A broomstick is placed or held out horizontally about one yard from the floor inside the circle. One by one the students dance, bending backward, under the stick, without touching the floor with their hands. After each round the stick is lowered by two inches. Who can dance the lowest without touching the stick or the floor?

Older   Teens

Centipede Dance

Age group: 10 and older

Requirements: rhythmic dance music

This is a short, simple chain dance suitable for playing in between two other activities. The players stand in a long line, one behind

the other. Each person puts his left arm between his legs and takes the right hand of the child behind him. The chain moves in circles or back and forth across the room to rhythmic dance music. Try to take one step for each beat.

Older   Teens

Spaghetti Dance

Age group: 8 and over

Requirements: dance music with a slow introduction

Tell the children that they are all pieces of uncooked, hard, straight spaghetti and that the room is the pan in which they are being cooked. To begin, they all lie on the floor, straight as a rod. Find music that has a slow buildup, or a piece with a long, slow introduction.

In the beginning they can only roll over, but as the water heats up the spaghetti becomes softer and the players start to "cook." As the music speeds up the pieces of spaghetti gradually become more supple. When the water boils they move more and more quickly back and forth, more and more wildly until the music stops. Then they sink down to the bottom of the pot once again.

Older **Teens**

Blindman's Polka

Age group: 10 and older

Requirements: 3 or 4 pieces of gentle dance music; empty space; blindfolds for half the group

Collect several recordings of mellow dance music. Half the players are blindfolded and have "sighted" partners. The sighted player takes the blindfolded player by the hand, and they dance together around the room. After about one minute the music changes to a different piece and the sighted players carefully pass their partners on to another sighted player. After another minute the music changes and the partners are changed again. After changing the music three or four times, the blindfolded players take off their blindfolds, the sighted players put them on, and the game begins again.

Older **Teens**

The **Drum Dance**

Age group: 8 and older

Requirements: a drum or tambourine for half the players

The children stand in two straight lines facing each other or in two circles, one inside the other. The game is played in pairs, so each child must have a partner opposite her. All the children in one row (or in the outer circle) have a drum or tambourine in their right

hands. The drum hangs down, and they swing it rhythmically back and forth. The other children have a drumstick in their right hands and beat the drum or tambourine once as it swings toward them.

Let the children practice for a few minutes. Once they have the hang of it, they can try doing it all together in the same tempo, also getting the drum beat at the same time. Then they can try beating the drum twice on alternate swings, so the rhythm becomes: swing-beat-swing-(rest)-swing-beatbeat-swing-(rest). Allow the group to experiment and come up with more variations; many are possible.

Relaxation Games

These relaxation games form a very special category. They are not educational games per se, in that they are not related to any specific subject or discipline; rather, they are simply intended to give the pupils a feeling of deep relaxation and as such can be used inside or outside school. They can be used well as an introduction to a lesson that requires a lot of concentration. After a relaxation exercise of ten to twenty minutes, it will be a great deal easier for the students to concentrate. Another use for these games is as a weekly half-hour relaxation period for children with learning or sleep problems.

These games are called musical relaxation games because their effect comes from carefully selected relaxing background music (sometimes called "New Age music"). This restful music is recommended for each game and should be played softly to strengthen the effect of the spoken text. Ideally the students should lie down in a pleasant, peaceful space for these exercises, but it is also possible to do them sitting on chairs.

Special Features

- The formula for most of these games is as follows: soft background music is played over which the leader reads the story in a soothing voice, slowly and with plenty of pauses.
- This form of musical activity is similar to what is called "guided fantasy."

Young   Older

The
Underwater Journey

Age group: 6–10

Requirements: New Age music with water sounds

Play a piece of very quiet New Age music, preferably one with water or ocean sounds. Keep the volume very low so that you can easily speak over it. The children can sit where they are and lay their heads on their arms on the desk. The whole journey can last just three or four minutes; as soon as the players hear the music, they close their eyes and you begin to speak the text below very slowly and quietly; the dots represent a few seconds' pause:

> This music enchants your breath so that you can breathe underwater, just like a mermaid. Breathe in deeply... and the enchantment begins to work... and very slowly you transform into a mermaid or merman.... (music)
>
> With each breath a part of your body changes... your legs grow together and become a tail... scales grow on your body... breathe in deeply again... and now you can swim underwater... let yourself sink down in the water and dive deeper and deeper down.... (music)
>
> Under the water it is light blue everywhere... you look around and see green plants swaying... you see brightly colored fish staring at you in wonder... you look down and see crabs walking along the sea bed, where shells lie everywhere.... (music)
>
> Now you slowly swim upward again, higher and higher until you put your head above the water. Now the enchantment begins to wear off, your scales disappear, and your tail turns back into legs. You swim to the beach and lie on the sand and open your eyes again.... (gradually fade the music out)

Young **Older**

A Springtime Walk

Age group: 6–10

Requirements: New Age music with birdsong

Put very relaxing New Age music on as a background, preferably one with birdsong, and tell the children that they are going to take a very special nature walk. The walk (and the music) will take about five minutes. The players can lay their heads on their arms and close their eyes as soon as the music begins.

Then slowly and softly you tell the following story, pausing wherever there are dots:

> Imagine that you are going for a quiet walk outside...but once you get outside you discover that everything has changed. You can see only woods, in front of you, all around you. The weather is fine, the sun is shining, and the birds are singing, so you decide to take a walk in the woods.... There is a small path through the trees, and you start off down that path.... (music)
>
> After you walk a little way, it becomes lighter and you see that the path comes out into a big meadow.... The meadow is full of long grass with blue and white flowers everywhere.... It looks so beautiful that you take off your shoes and socks and run barefoot through the grass....
>
> Now you can smell the scent of the flowers...see beautiful butterflies you have never seen before...yellow, blue, purple, and orange butterflies...you gaze in wonder at all the butterflies and walk slowly on through the meadow... you see marvelous flowers you've never seen before.... (music)

But now you have to go back, and with your shoes in your hands you find your way back to the path.... You put your shoes and socks on again and follow the path through the woods...as you go, you listen to the singing of all the birds in the trees...after a little while you come to the edge of the woods, and suddenly there is the school right in front of you.... You go quietly back inside, go to your place, and open your eyes again.... (slowly fade out the music)

Older Teens

The House in the Woods

Age group: 10 and older

Requirements: New Age music

Everyone relaxes with eyes closed in their chairs or lying on their backs on the ground. Play some very soft New Age music as a background and tell this story in a quiet, soothing voice:

It is summer; imagine that you are drifting on the ocean, somewhere far away. The sea is calm and peaceful, the water is cold, but the sun shines above you, making you feel warm and relaxed. You float on your back, letting yourself be carried on the waves....

After a little while you are washed up on a beach and you crawl out of the water. You lie on the warm, soft sand. You are completely alone....

You look around you and see that there is a wood at the top of the beach. When you have dried off, you slowly walk toward the woods. You see a narrow path leading into the woods. You go into the woods where it is very quiet and peaceful, where all you can hear is the singing of birds....

After walking through the woods a little way you come out by a stream; you see a little wooden bridge crossing it. The path splits into two at this point: one path leads to the right along the stream, the other leads straight ahead over the bridge. You decide to cross the bridge, and you hear your footsteps on the wood and the rushing of water....

Then you stand still: a little way in front of you there is a clearing, and you see a large house, old and tumbling down. You go toward it and wonder whether to go inside. It looks a little scary. You decide to go in anyway. You try the front door, but it is locked. You walk around and try the back door. It opens with a loud creak. Hesitantly you go inside....

After about 10 seconds, the leader can play a few soft notes or melodies on a glockenspiel. Then slowly fade out the music and ask the students to open their eyes.

What did they see in the house? Let everyone tell his or her experiences.

Teens

A Musical Trip Around the World

Age group: 12 and older; not too large a group

Requirements: paper and drawing materials for all the players

This game is best played in a large space or gym, but if necessary it can be done in the classroom. Each student has a sheet of paper and a pencil or felt tip pen. Prerecord four fragments of restful, atmospheric music, each about one and a half to two minutes long. The pieces of music should be quite different from one another; here are some suggestions:

1. "Morning" from *Peer Gynt* by Grieg
2. "The Swan" from *The Carnival of the Animals* by Saint-Saëns
3. "Silk Road Suite" by Kitaro
4. "Winter" from *The Four Seasons* by Vivaldi

We are now going to take a trip around the world, visiting four different countries. We board an airplane and fly to the first country. With the leader as tour guide the group goes slowly to the first corner in the room. On the way the tour guide tells them that they are going to a country where they have never been before. They have to try to discover for themselves what country they are in by listening to the music. It is not an existing country, but a fantasyland.

When the children arrive, they sit in a circle on the floor and divide their paper into four parts. The parts are numbered one to four. Tell them that they will now hear a piece of music and should imagine a landscape in which this music fits. Is it warm or cold, are there mountains or is it flat, is there an ocean or a forest, is it daytime or night? Then they close their eyes and listen to the first piece of music. When it is over the tour guide repeats the questions and the students draw their imaginary landscape in the first part.

They have only two to three minutes for this, so it has to be a quick sketch.

Then everyone stands up, taking the paper with them, and sets off in the plane for the next country—in other words they follow the tour guide to another corner of the room. There they hear the second piece of music, the same questions are asked, and in the second part of the paper they sketch a landscape that suits this new music.

After visiting the four corners of the room, the teacher leads the players in a discussion of their drawings. Remember: there are no right or wrong pictures.

Older **Teens**

Head Seeks Tummy

Age group: 10 and older

Requirements: an empty space

The children lie on their backs on the floor, each one with their head on the tummy of another. Once in position they should all be linked together like dominoes. This position will at first give rise to plenty of giggling. Don't stop the children giggling, but point out that each time they laugh, they are bouncing someone else's head up and down with their tummies!

When they have settled down, tell them that each child can feel the other's breathing, because when one breathes in and out, the other's head will go up and down. Each child tries to breathe in the

same rhythm as the child on whose tummy her head is resting. After a short time the whole group will be breathing in the same rhythm. We can hear this if everyone breathes out with an "ah" sound.

Teens

Music with the Whole Body

Age group: 12 and older

Requirements: New Age or synthesizer music

Play some relaxing but impressive music, for example, "Oxygene" or "Equinoxe" by J. M. Jarre or "Silk Road Suite" by Kitaro. Ask the students to relax in their chairs or to lie on the ground. Play the music softly. Slowly, and with plenty of pauses, tell them this story:

> We hear music not only with our ears—our whole body can feel the reverberation of the music. If you listen consciously, you will feel the music in your body as well. (ten seconds of music)
>
> Try to sit or lie as still as you can.... Feel the places where your body makes contact with the chair [or the floor].... Now turn your hands so your palms face upward. These are the dishes into which the sounds of the music are poured. When you listen to the music now, try to catch it in your hands (thirty seconds of music).
>
> Now try to draw the music into your chest and abdomen....
>
> Now try to feel the music in your whole body. Be totally open to the music.... Feel it vibrating through your whole body.... The music pours into you and out again, through you, washing all around you....
>
> (The music is slowly faded out.)
>
> Let the music echo inside you.... Move your fingers, reach out your arms, and stretch your whole body.... Now gradually open your eyes.

Multicultural and Intercultural Games

In many schools, intercultural or multicultural education is still marginal, being generally limited to celebrating the festivals of other cultures and an annual "multicultural day." There are, however, countless simple solutions to make education in various fields more multicultural.

This section of the book includes examples of multicultural games. In addition, many games in which Western music is used can be made intercultural by substituting dance music from another culture. The game itself can remain otherwise unchanged, since games are universal. For example, the Instruments Dance (game 33 in *101 Music Games for Children*) can be played just as well with salsa music as with Western pop music. The same applies to games like Hat Dance, Living Mirror, Tableau Vivant, and Leading and Following from the *101 Music Games for Children* and for more or less all dance and movement games.

As an exception, in this section we have used three well-known foreign folk songs as the basis for dance games. It is usually better to use familiar melodies because it is very difficult to learn unfamiliar foreign songs. You can substitute here whatever cultures are most prevalent in your country. We have also included three folk stories from Turkey, Morocco, and Surinam (West Africa), with the purpose of turning them into sound stories. That means that all the sounds featuring in the story have to be made by the children using their instruments and voices. The teacher tells the story, and wherever sounds occur, marked by (...), she pauses and some of the children produce the relevant sounds. So the story has to be told at least twice: the first time to look for appropriate instruments and rehearse the sounds, and the second time for real.

Older

The Multicultural Circle Dance

Age group: 8–12

Requirements: recordings of four or more pieces of music

Ask the students to suggest or bring from home music recordings representative of their country (or state) of origin. Each musical excerpt should last approximately two minutes. Select four or more pieces of music from the various national and cultural groups represented in the class.

Divide the class into groups, one for each piece of music chosen with the student whose music was chosen as the leader of the group and the others as followers. The leader makes a simple dance to the musical selection—perhaps using dance steps or movements from her culture—and teaches it to the rest of the group. This way a dance is designed for every one of the selections.

Once the leaders have taught their group the various dances, assemble the children into a circle. Ask the leader from one group to walk to the center of the circle and perform his or her dance while the musical selection is playing. The followers join in the dance from their places in the circle, and the others join in when they feel ready. Do the same for the second, third, and following selections. Whose dance is the easiest to "follow"? Whose is the most challenging? Let the class talk about what they enjoyed and found difficult.

Older

Multilingual Canon

Age group: 8–12

Duration: 15–20 minutes

The well-known French song "Le coq est mort" also has English and Spanish versions: "My Rooster Died Yesterday" and "Mi gallo se murió ayer." You can adapt the songs to suit the different cultures in your group.

Teach the Spanish version to the children, soliciting help from any native speakers if possible. If they repeat the last line, it can be sung in a canon with the other languages. Divide the rest of the class into two groups and teach one half the English version and the other the French. Then let the children sing the song in a canon in the three different languages. What does it sound like in three languages simultaneously? For more variety, ask the children to translate the song into other languages they speak.

My roos-ter died____ yes-ter-day.   My roos-ter died____ yes-ter-day.
Mi gal-lo se mur - io a - yer.   Mi gal-lo se mur - io a - yer.
Le coq est mort, le coq est mort.   Le coq est mort, le coq est mort.

Now he can-not sing co-co - re, co-co-ra.   Now he can-not sing co-co - re, co-co-ra.
Ya - no can-ta - re co-co - ri, co-co-ra.   Ya - no can-ta - re co-co - ri, co-co-ra.
Il ne di - ra plus co-co - di, co-co-da.   Il ne di - ra plus co-co - di, co-co-da.

Co - co - co - co re,   co - co - re,   co - ra.
Co - co - co - co - ri,   co - co - ri,   co - ra.
Co - co di - co di - co,____   di - co da.

Older

Multicultural Song Festival

Age group: 8–12

Requirements: rhythm instruments

This game requires advance preparation of one or two weeks and could be used in conjunction with a special day or school spirit event. Well before the date of the activity, ask who among the children would like to sing a popular or traditional song from their country or culture of origin. Some children may also want to sing a song from a different country or culture that is not represented in the class, and that is fine. The children can also sing in pairs.

Ask the children who do not want to sing if they would like to accompany the singers on simple rhythm or melody instruments; give all of them time to practice accompanying the singers in their songs. Ask the children who are not singing or accompanying others to form small groups to compose short percussion interludes to be played in between songs.

The performance begins with a singer announcing the song and explaining what it is about, then the singer or his or her "group" performs the song. This may be followed by a percussion piece. At the end of the percussion piece, another student begins his or her song, and so on until all the singers have finished.

Older

An English and a Turkish Fox

Age group: 8–10

Duration: 15–20 minutes

First teach the children the English version, then the Turkish. The Turkish text is almost the same as the English, except that it is about ducks rather than ganders.

Divide the class into two: one half sings, the others play the game.

For this game at least half of the room should be empty. First a fox is chosen. The fox can be given a special hat. The rest of the players are divided into two: one group of geese, one group of farmers. The geese make a circle but don't hold hands. The farmers form another circle and hold hands. They must not let go hands during the game.

Start with the English version.

At a signal from the teacher the singers begin singing the song: both circles walk around in time to the music. The fox stays still until the song is over then tries to catch a goose. Meanwhile, the farmers try to capture the fox in their circle—without letting go hands. The game is over if the fox catches a goose or if the fox is caught by the farmers. Once the fox is in the farmers' circle, he cannot escape.

Then choose a different child to be fox and let the singers sing the Turkish version. The geese and farmers should change places, and the game can begin again. After playing these two versions, let the singers play the game while the other players become singers. Then play both versions of the game again.

Fox, you've sto - len   my gray gan - der,   bet - ter bring him   back,
Til - ki ka - zi   ne - den cal - din   ver - o - nu - ge   ri,

bet - ter bring him   back!   There's a   hun - ter   watch-ing yon - der,
ver - o - nu - ge   ri   e - ger ca - buk   ge - tir - mez - sen

He   is   on   your   track._____   There's   a   hun - ter
tu - ta   rim   se - ni_____   e - ger   ca - buk

wat - ching   yon - der,   he   is   on   your   track.
ge - tir - mez - sen   tu - ta - rim   se - ni.

87

Young

Orchestra Game

Age group: 6–9

Requirements: rhythm instruments

Duration: 10–15 minutes

Play a recording of a song from another country, any song with a clear, regular rhythm. The group sits in a circle; in the center are as many rhythm instruments as possible. Pass the instruments out one by one and let the children join in one by one, playing the rhythm or the time of the song—softly, otherwise you won't be able to hear the music. When everyone is playing the teacher points to one child, who then stops playing. The teacher keeps doing this until only one child is left playing. When the music stops, the last child stops too.

Then play the same game with a song from another country.

Young

La Pulga de San Jose: Latin American Song with Movements

Age group: younger children

First, teach the English and the Spanish versions of the first verse of "La Pulga de San Jose"/"The Market of San Jose" to the children. Tell the children that each verse of the song contains a different instrument, and have the children demonstrate hand motions for each of the five instruments: a guitar (pretend to strum a guitar); a clarinet (hold hands in front of the body and wiggle the fingers as though pressing on clarinet keys); a violin (hold one arm down and use the other one to mime a violin bow); a cello (use one hand to pretend to hold the stem and the other to bow the cello across the midsection of the body); and a drum (pretend to play on bongo drums).

Next, sing the song in English all the way through, having the children demonstrate the hand motions for each of the instruments in turn. Then sing the Spanish version, doing the same hand motions. During the chorus for both versions, have the children clap the rhythm of the song. When singing the Spanish version, try to use correct Spanish pronunciation. The instrument vowel sounds (guitarra, clarinete, violín, violón, and tumtum) progress through the Spanish vowels (ah, eh, ee, oh, oo).

"La Pulga de San Jose * The Flea Market of San Jose," from DIEZ DEDITOS by Jose-Luis Orozco, copyright (c) 1997 by Jose-Luis Orozco, text and musical arrangements. Used by permission of Dutton Children's Books, an imprint of Penguin Putnam Books for Young Readers, a division of Penguin Putnam Inc.

In the market of San Jose
I bought a clarinet,
net, net, net, the clarinet,
tarra, tarra, tarra, the guitar.

You can go...

In the market of San Jose
I bought a violin,
lin, lin, the violin,
net, net, net, the clarinet,
tarra, tarra, tarra, the guitar.

You can go...

In the market of San Jose
I bought a cello,
low, low, the cello,
lin, lin, the violin,
net, net, net, the clarinet,
tarra, tarra, tarra, the guitar.

You can go...

In the market of San Jose
I bought a drum,
tum, tum, the drum,
low, low, the cello,
lin, lin, the violin,
net, net, net, the clarinet,
tarra, tarra, tarra, the guitar.

You can go...

En la Pulga de San José
yo compré un clarinete,
nete, nete, nete, el clarinete,
tarra, tarra, tarra, la guitarra.

Vaya usted...

En la Pulga de San José
yo compré un violín,
lín, lín, el violín,
nete, nete, nete, el clarinete,
tarra, tarra, tarra, la guitarra.

Vaya usted...

En la Pulga de San José
yo compré un violón,
lón, lón, el violín,
lín, lín, el violín,
nete, nete, nete, el clarinete,
tarra, tarra, tarra, la guitarra.

Vaya usted...

En la Pulga de San José
yo compré un tumtum,
tum, tum, el tumtum,
lón, lón, el violín,
lín, lín, el violín,
nete, nete, nete, el clarinete,
tarra, tarra, tarra, la guitarra.

Vaya usted...

Circle Game from Curaçao

Age group: 6–8

Translation: Let's make a circle dance,
who will we choose?

The children stand in a circle holding hands, with one child standing in the middle. They walk around in time with the song. When the song is over, the child in the center chooses a partner. They hold hands, and when the singing starts again they dance around in the opposite direction of the big circle. When the singing stops, the second child in the circle chooses a new partner to join them, and now the three of them form a small circle in the middle. This continues so that the inner circle gets larger while the outer circle gets smaller. When it becomes impossible to fit anyone more in the inner circle without breaking hands in the outer circle, the game is over. (This game is similar to Farmer in the Dell).

Older **Teens**

The Big Slap: A Surinamese/West African Sound Story

Age group: 8 and older

Requirements: an assortment of instruments

In a sound story, part of the class has instruments and illustrates the sounds featured in the story.

First make an inventory of all the sounds. In this case they are footsteps, storm sounds, thunder and lightning, rain, knocks on the door, and a big bang. Figure out who will make these sounds, and with which instruments, and then tell the following story. A row of dots indicates the places at which the sounds should be made.

> One morning, spider Anansi woke up and cheerfully left his house in search of something to eat.... But suddenly dark clouds rolled up and a storm began.... It was Mr. Thunder, who always made a lot of noise and could make it rain very hard....
>
> "Why is he doing that?" asked Anansi "Doesn't he know I'm walking here?" So he shouted, "Hey, Thunder, don't make such a noise when I'm out walking! Don't you have any respect for me?'
>
> Mr. Thunder was very offended. In the first place, he was always supposed to be addressed as Mr. Thunder, and in the second place, he wasn't going to take any nonsense from a stupid spider. He made the thunder extra loud...so that the earth shook and the trees blew wildly back and forth making cracking sounds.... But Anansi pretended not to be afraid. He thought he was the smartest spider in the whole world.

"Anansi," called Mr. Thunder, "Who are you that you dare to defy me? Why should I respect you?'

Now Anansi become very angry and decided to teach Thunder a lesson. The braggart! "You're just a windbag, and you can't scare me!" cried Anansi, and stamped all eight of his feet on the ground....

"Oh yes?" shouted Mr. Thunder, "Are you mad, Anansi? If I give you a slap, your head's going to end up miles away. Ha!"

"We'll see about that!" yelled Anansi in fury. "A slap from you won't hurt me. You know what? Why don't you come to my house at four o'clock tomorrow morning, then you can give me a slap. Do you dare to do that?'

"To your house?" thundered Mr. Thunder. "Of course I dare, and I'll slap you so hard your head will come off. Tomorrow morning I'll be there!"

And with a whole lot of thunder and hubbub Mr. Thunder stormed off into the clouds....

Anansi was wet through from the rain, so he ran home as fast as he could to get dry.... When he realized what he'd done by challenging Mr. Thunder like that, he began to get just a little bit scared. He would never survive a slap from Mr. Thunder; it would be the death of him. But Anansi was a clever spider, so he thought up a plan. He ran to Brother Rooster and knocked on the door....

"Brother Rooster, my best friend, can I invite you to dinner tonight? I've got lots of rum!"

Brother Rooster loved rum, so he happily accepted the invitation. Anansi cooked a wonderful meal, and thanks to the rum they had a very good time....

When Brother Rooster wanted to go home, Anansi stopped him, saying, "Why don't you stay. We've still got so much to talk about, and we haven't finished the rum yet. You can stay the night." Brother Rooster let himself be persuaded. Anansi had just one more request: "I can't get up early, and the milkman comes at 4:00 A.M. Would you open the door when he knocks?"

"Certainly, " said Brother Rooster, "I always rise early, even before the sun." And they both went to sleep....

But Anansi stayed awake so he could watch what happened. At 4:00 there was a loud knock at the door. The whole house shook.... It was still quite dark outside. Brother Rooster woke up and opened the door.... There was a huge bang, and Brother Rooster lay dead on the floor....

"That'll teach you," snarled Mr. Thunder, and he stomped back into the clouds.... Because it was so dark he didn't see that he'd slapped the wrong person. Some time later, Anansi had plucked the rooster, dressed it, and made it ready for the oven. Then he went outside and called Mr. Thunder, who was astonished. "Are you still alive? Then I didn't slap you hard enough. How would you like another slap tomorrow morning?"

Anansi still thought he was the smartest spider in the whole world and accepted the challenge. He could use the same trick again. This time he invited Brother Tiger. Brother Tiger just loved roasted rooster, so he was delighted to accept the invitation. Brother Tiger also allowed himself to be persuaded to stay the night and open the door for the milkman....

At four o'clock there was again a loud knock at the door.... Brother Tiger opened it, and there was another big bang.... Brother Tiger was struck dead on the spot. Anansi buried the tiger in his garden, and a little later he went outside again and called Mr. Thunder. Mr. Thunder was beside himself with fury, thundering, and raging...and agreed with Anansi that the following morning he would come for the third and last time to give him a slap.

Again Anansi went in search of a guest. This time it was Brother Leopard. After dinner he was also asked to stay the night and open the door for the milkman. But Brother Leopard knew that Anansi didn't drink milk, and he didn't trust him. He pretended to go to sleep and snored loudly.... Anansi was sure that everything would go according to plan, and he fell asleep.... Then Brother Leopard crept quietly outside and hid behind a tree. At four o'clock Mr. Thunder came and knocked on the door again..., but no one opened the door. He knocked again, and Anansi woke up...and searched the whole house but couldn't find Brother Leopard anywhere. "Open up, Anansi, or I'll knock the door down!" boomed Mr. Thunder with a great hullabaloo.... But Anansi silently sneaked out of the back door and stayed out of sight. Finally he understood that you can't play the same trick three times!

Older **Teens**

The Prophet: A Middle-Eastern Sound Story

Age group: 10 and older

First make a list of all the sounds in this story about the folk hero Nasruddin: donkey's footsteps, chopping wood, cracking branches, people's footsteps, a donkey braying, and the creaking lid of a chest. Pass out the instruments and decide who makes what sound.

> Nasruddin needed some firewood, so he took his donkey and rode off into the woods.... There he climbed into a tree and started to chop off a large branch with his axe.... A stranger passing by heard the noise, looked up, and saw to his amazement that Nasruddin was sitting on the branch he was trying to chop off....

"Friend," he called, "if you carry on like that you're going to fall!"

Nasruddin took no notice of the warning and went on chopping . . . until the branch broke off with a crack and fell to the ground, taking Nasruddin with it . . . .

Dazed, Nasruddin pulled himself to his feet and ran after the stranger, who had walked on . . . . "Sir," he called, "I think you must be a prophet because you predicted that I would fall from the tree. But can you also predict when I will die?'

The stranger didn't want to waste a lot of time on someone who behaved so stupidly, so to be rid of him he said, "When your donkey brays twice, then you will die."

Nasruddin was very troubled about this and walked despondently back to the tree . . . . He loaded the wood onto the donkey's back and trudged back to the village . . . .

Halfway back, the donkey brayed twice . . . and Nasruddin immediately felt ill. He turned as white as a sheet and fainted in fear . . . . After a little while two villagers found him lying there. He had turned so pale that they thought he was dead. They brought a wooden chest, laid him in it, and closed the lid . . . . Next they carried him carefully to the village. . . . But at the crossroads they started to argue about which was the quickest way to his house. The movement of the chest had revived Nasruddin, who heard them wrangling about the shortest route. Suddenly he pushed open the lid of the chest with a loud creak and sat up . . . . "The shortest way is to the left, and hurry up or I'll be late for dinner!"

The villagers let out a scream and ran away as fast as they could . . . .

Older

The Impossible Task: A Moroccan Sound Story

Age group: 8–12

Requirements: instruments for all the players

This is an old Arabic story with an important moral that is well known in Morocco. First list the sounds which come into the story and let the children practice making them (footsteps of a man and a donkey, the sound of pieces of broken pottery, the sound of fireworks, drums, water). Then tell this story (the children make the appropriate noises at the dots).

> A man had lost all his money as the result of an accident, and he lived in great poverty. At his wits' end, he went to a famous magician who lived in a nearby town and knocked on his door.... The magician asked what he wanted. The man asked him if he could help him get as many pieces of gold as possible as quickly as he could. The magician pondered deeply and gave him the following advice:
>
> "Collect as many pieces of broken pottery as you can. Wait until the day of the Ashura Festival, because that is the only day on which this magic works, and throw the pieces into the well outside the village. Then they will change into pieces of gold. But be careful! Don't think about a hare, otherwise it won't work, and you will have to wait to try again until next year."
>
> The man thanked the magician and returned home.... There he started to break as many bowls and pots as he could find... and put the pieces into baskets.... Then he waited impatiently for the Ashura Festival. Finally the day

arrived. He loaded all his baskets on the backs of donkeys...and with a string of at least ten donkeys, he set off for the well....

On the way he came across children everywhere, celebrating the Festival of Ashura. Some of the boys threw crackers...; little girls walked with their dolls, which were dressed as brides and bridegrooms, and other children beat all kinds of drums....

But the man took no notice, and left the village with his donkeys..., dreaming of all that gold! At last he came to the well, unloaded the baskets, and threw all the shards of pottery into the well... just as the magician had told him to do. At that moment he suddenly remembered that the magician had also told him not to think about a hare! Too late! He had just thought of one. Furious, he ran to the magician's house...and knocked on the door....

"Your advice is impossible to follow!" he cried. "If I think that I mustn't think about a hare, I've already thought about it and everything goes wrong!"

The magician laughed and said, "You asked me something impossible. All I could do was give you an impossible answer." The man walked home angrily...while the children in the village continued to celebrate Ashura....

Game Projects

The game projects in this section are extended forms of expression games: they are based on themes, such as the circus, a fairground, the four seasons, and so on. Choose a project game if you desire a more project-oriented approach, that is, when lessons are devoted to a specific subject for a longer period or for several short periods. This might be the case with theme weeks, creativity weeks, school camps, and so on.

These projects require a good selection of instruments, and the leaders should preferably have some experience with musical expression games.

Special Features

- Game projects are intended to help to develop musical creativity.
- Game projects offer the opportunity for continuing on one subject for two, three, four, or more lessons so that the various parts of the project can be worked out more deeply and fully.
- Along with musical education, social education is also highlighted in these games through the high degree of cooperation and collaboration required of the students.

93

Older

1 or 2 x ½ hrs

Circus Project

Age group: 8–12

Requirements: instruments for all the players; rope; sticky tape; paper; hoop

On the ground is a large circle made with rope or sticky tape, representing a circus ring. The children sit inside the circle. To create a circus atmosphere, ask the children what kinds of animals are in a circus. Begin with a guessing game: Who can make the sound of one of the animals? The rest of the class guesses what animal it is. After the most important animals have been mentioned, you can change the children into some of them.

In advance you have prepared pieces of paper with the names of four circus animals: elephants, lions, horses, and chimpanzees. There must be as many pieces of paper as there are children, and the total should be divisible by four so that there are an equal number of each animal. Put all the notes in a hat. Each child draws one, reads it, and folds it again. Then put on some cheerful circus music and have each child walk or dance around like the animal whose name they drew. So if they drew "elephant," they should imitate its heavy, lumbering steps; if a horse, its canter; if a lion, its prowl; and if a chimpanzee, its jump (for example).

The children move around in time to the music, each as their own animal, watching what the others do; when they see other animals the same as themselves, they group together; an elephant seeks out the other elephants and they form a group, a lion finds the other lions, and so forth. Within one or two minutes you will end up with four groups of animals. As soon as the four groups are formed, turn off the music.

The Parade

Every circus begins with a parade of all the animals. We will begin with the elephants. Divide the elephants into two groups (by counting off one-two-one-two). The ones sit in the center of the circle and form an elephant orchestra; the twos form a line outside the circle and walk around the circle like elephants to the music played by the orchestra. What would elephant music sound like? It would sound heavy and lumbering, so have the children use drums and heavy-sounding instruments. (Think of the elephants in *The Jungle Book;* the players may want to use that march rhythm). The leader also plays in the orchestra and indicates when they should start and stop. After one circuit of the ring, the march of the elephants is over.

The elephants sit down in the circle, and it is the horses' turn. Proceed as above: half the group sits in the middle playing horse music, and the others walk round the ring being horses. How would horse music sound? Preferably use wooden instruments and bells to imitate the sounds of cantering horses. After a round of the

horse dance come the lions. Lion music would be rather jungly! Choose drums and so forth to make exciting rhythmic jungle music. The lions prowl around, growling fiercely.

Finally come the chimpanzees. For chimpanzee music, use maracas and other shakers, to make the chimpanzees leap around happily. After each round there should, of course, be a burst of applause from the rest of the group!

The Circus Acts

Now it's time for the individual acts. Divide the whole class into two groups: the elephants and horses are one group and become the circus orchestra. The lions and chimpanzees become group two and begin with their acts.

The circus orchestra (group one) must first learn to play a crescendo on the instruments (whatever they may choose). At a signal from the leader they begin quietly and gradually to build up the volume until they finish at their loudest with a crash of cymbals played by the teacher. Once they have learned to do this, they can accompany the other group's act.

Group two now plays the elephants. Each child takes a chair in the ring and stands on it on hands and feet. While the music begins softly, the players slowly climb onto their chairs, and while the music swells, they stand on one leg, with trunks in the air. They remain like this until the music reaches a crescendo, and as the cymbals clash they all jump down to the ground. Then the groups switch; the elephants become the orchestra, and the orchestra become elephants.

Next come the horses. For this part of the game, the groups change over again, with the orchestra becoming horses and the elephants becoming the orchestra again.

Under the leader's direction, the orchestra plays a cheerful, even rhythm (for example, the beginning of "Jingle Bells"). The other group forms pairs: the larger (or stronger) partner is the horse, the other the rider. The rider jumps on the horse's back, and the horse holds its rider firmly by the legs. The horses now canter around with their riders, in time to the music, now and then making a graceful turn. After a few rounds the cymbals sound, and the riders dismount. Then the groups change places, and the orchestra has a turn at being horses and riders.

Next come the lions. The groups change over again: the orchestra is now lions jumping through a hoop, the horses become the orchestra. For this part you need a hoop or a bicycle tire and a mattress. Two children hold the hoop about a foot and a half above the ground in front of the mattress. The lions stand in a line a few yards from the hoop. As the orchestra plays a short crescendo, each lion in turn runs up, and as the cymbals clash, jumps through the hoop and falls on the mattress. This activity will need to be rehearsed to get the timing right. The crescendo will be short, because the run up to the hoop is short. This must be clearly signaled by the leader. Then the groups change places again.

Finally come the chimpanzees, with their tightrope dance. The lions are now the orchestra, and the orchestra members are the chimpanzees. The orchestra plays glockenspiels and xylophones, tuned pentatonically, and improvise melodies, accompanied by some rattles. The chimpanzees walk one by one with an open umbrella in one hand and with their toes on the rope, which is stuck to the floor. When they get to the end of the rope, there is a clash of cymbals and they jump down, giving the umbrella to the next chimpanzee.

The project can be concluded by playing the circus music you used at the beginning and by having everyone do their own animal dance.

Older

1 or 2 x ½ hrs

Fairground Project

Age group: 8–12

Requirements: instruments for all the players; barrel-organ music

Duration: 1 hour or 2 half-hour lessons

In this project you will make a musical rendition of four fairground attractions:

- bumper cars
- merry-go-round
- shooting gallery
- haunted house

Bumper cars. Make a large circle on the floor, using rope, chalk, or sticky tape. Four children stand in the circle and play at being bumper cars. The other children remain outside the circle. The bumper cars stand side-by-side, one pair on each side of the circle. One pair goes around the circle forward, in a counterclockwise direction, the other pair goes backward in a clockwise direction. They can crash into each other, but should try to avoid it. In the middle are two children with instruments—they drive the cars. One child might have a drum that drives the children going forward. As long as the drum plays, the two cars move forward in small steps. The other child might have a triangle: as long as the triangle sounds, the other two children move backward in small steps. When no one is playing, the "cars" stand still, holding a cushion over their tummies with crossed arms. After a few rounds, four other children can be the cars and two new children become the "drivers." It is also possible for all four bumper cars to have their own "driver": in this case you must have four children in the center, each with a different instrument.

Merry-go-round. This merry-go-round has several horses that go up and down and some cars that turn around. Choose two or three children to play the horses and two or three to be the cars. These four or six stand equidistant around the circumference of the circle, just as on a real merry-go-round. The horses and cars are driven by two children with different instruments standing in the center of the circle. One child might have a glockenspiel: each time she plays a chime on the glockenspiel, the horses, who go around on hands and feet, go up and down. To do this they "rear up," standing just on their feet, then go back to hands and feet. The children playing the cars walk around normally, and each time their driver plays his instrument (for example, rattles a tambourine) they turn around once or twice as they walk.

The merry-go-round is set in motion when the leader puts on some barrel-organ music; the children walk around gently, all in the same direction. Place the horses and cars alternately: car-horse-car, at equal distances from one another. As they go around, they should keep these distances equal. After a few minutes choose different children to be horses, cars, and drivers. Here again you can have different "drivers" for each individual horse and car, each with a different instrument.

Shooting-gallery. For a musical illustration of shooting, place five empty cans or small cardboard boxes on a table. The cans should be marked with the names of notes: C, D, E, F, G.

On a side table are a xylophone and hammer. This game can only be played by one child at a time. She "shoots" by closing her eyes and playing one note on the xylophone. The teacher looks to see which note it was and removes the corresponding can. If she hits another note, or between notes, she misses. Each child can shoot five times per turn. How many hits do they get? After five shots, it's the next child's turn. Who ends up with the highest score?

Haunted house. First write five kinds of scary noises on the blackboard—the sort of sounds you might hear in a haunted house at the fairground, for example:

- rattling skeletons
- ghost sounds
- monster sounds
- witches screeching
- scary animal sounds (snakes hissing, for example)

Form five groups of three or four children and have them spend a short time practicing the sounds listed on the board; one group makes skeleton sounds, another makes ghost sounds, and so on. The players can use their voices or instruments, which can be played in unusual ways. The sounds should be as weird and scary as possible. Once they have tried this out, each group takes up position in different parts of the room. Then they should be quite quiet. They can only make a sound when someone comes near them.

Who dares to go into the haunted house? A few volunteers are given tickets. They are blindfolded and are led slowly, one by one, through the house by a guide (one of the other children). The tour begins with a deathly hush, but as soon as someone comes near one of the groups, they let loose with their noises. When the people move away they fall silent again. While people are between groups it should be completely silent for a moment—this makes the experience much more exciting!

95

Teens

1¹/₂ to 2 hrs

World Music Festival

Age group: 12 and older

Requirements: instruments for all the players and four recordings of music from different cultures

Duration: 1¹/₂ to 2 hours

This project is particularly suitable for a creativity afternoon, as part of a school camp, or as a thematic week in which an introduction to other cultures plays a central role. You will need as many different kinds of musical instruments as possible.

Divide the class into four equal groups of four or five people. There must be at least four (or more) children left over for the game to work right.

Each group is given a "continent" and told that they will make musical sounds that are typically associated with that continent.

The "Africa" group uses drums (timpani, congas, drums, etc.) to make music with a strong, continuous drum rhythm.

The "Asia" group uses glockenspiels, metallophones, and xylophones to play pentatonic improvisations.

The "South America" group uses various small rhythm instruments (maracas, bongos, woodblocks, guïros, tambourines, etc.) to make music with a light, swinging dance rhythm (tango, rhumba, calypso, or something of the sort).

The "Europe" group should have melodic instruments if available, and if the participants can play them (keyboards, recorder, accordion, guitar, piano). Alternatively, they can sing or play well-known Western songs or melodies.

Each group has 15 minutes in which to practice playing in the style of their continent according to ideas given below.

The "Africa" group could play a strong, continuous, basic rhythm on two large drums with variations and counter-rhythms played on smaller drums.

The "Asia" group takes all the F's and B's off their instruments, leaving only a pentatonic scale. They then improvise on this scale.

The "South American" music should sound light and swinging, with counter-rhythms and syncopation on wooden and metal rhythm instruments.

The "European" group plays or sings a well-known song ("Early One Morning," "Ode to Joy") or a two-part canon ("Shalom," "London's Burning").

The Performance

Now the four continents hold a musical contest in which the aim is to encourage as many spectators as possible to join their group.

This is done as follows: the four continents go to sit in the four corners of the room. A volunteer from the group of spectators goes to sit in the middle of the room and closes his eyes. The leader indicates which group should play when, and each group plays in turn. After they have all finished playing, the listener chooses which music he liked best and goes to join that group. The group has now won a member, who can join in playing the music in the next round. This process is repeated with the next volunteer from the spectator's group and continues until all the participants are attached to a group.

The nice thing about this game is that a group whose music is less attractive to the spectators will play better and more beautifully with each new round, in order to increase the strength of their group.

Variations: After each group has played in their own style, see if two or three of the groups can find a way to play together. Discuss what happens. You can also create groups for more continents, and even imaginary ones.

Older   **Teens**

2 to 3 hrs

The Four Seasons

Age group: 10 and older

Requirements: roll of wallpaper; felt pens; instruments for all the players; a recording of Vivaldi's *Four Seasons*

This project is a piece of instant music theater that could be performed in class after one or two lessons, but is also an excellent basis for a thoroughly rehearsed performance on a parent's evening or summer camp. In either event, it requires two to three hours of intensive preparation. The group should be familiar with making sound collages (see, for instance, the expression games in this book) and with working independently in small groups.

The class is divided into four groups, each of which works on one season. Explain that each group is to prepare a drawing and a piece of music with movement depicting one of the four seasons. You can, of course, explain how the famous Italian composer, Antonio Vivaldi, did this in the form of four concerti. They are still in the classical "top ten," even today.

Start by making large group paintings. For this you will have already written on the board a few key words for each season to give the participants a guideline to build on. These words could come from asking, "When you think about spring/summer/autumn/winter, what are the first words that come to your mind?" Asking this question could result in this kind of list:

Spring: birdsong, young flowers and plants blooming, blossoms on the trees

Summer: warm, hot, vacations, swimming, baseball

Autumn: falling leaves, wind, storm, rain

Winter: cold, freezing, shivering, skating, throwing snowballs

Each group is given a large sheet of paper, and each member of the group draws something connected with their season, using felt pens or chalks. In the "spring group," one child might draw a big tree covered with blossoms; another might draw birds, another plants and flowers, and another nests with eggs in it, and so on. Point out that the group drawings should have a sense of coherence and that the elements should be as large as possible. They can also be colored in later on.

While the children are drawing, play the beginnings of each of the movements in Vivaldi's *Four Seasons* (about five minutes per season) and tell them which part they are listening to. Let them continue drawing as long as the music is playing (about twenty minutes), then they can complete their drawings by coloring them in so that they can later be used as colorful backdrops for the performance. The explanation, finding key words, and making the drawings will take about forty-five minutes, enough for one lesson.

The second lesson begins with making a kind of stage on which the children can perform. If necessary this stage could simply be a clear space in the room with two children holding up a sheet or a curtain as a screen or backdrop. Next, the four drawings are hung in turn, and once again the class is asked to suggest key words, but this time only relating to sounds. For example, from the spring drawing, birdsong, baby chicks peeping, leaves rustling, a stream rippling, and so on.

When this has been done, the class is again divided into the four seasons, and each group goes to its own corner of the room to try to reproduce the sounds on musical instruments and with their voices in the form of a sound collage. Each group should also split into two, half of them performing the sounds, the other making suitable movements, which could be in the form of a dance, a mime, or a more realistic act involving props (for example, having flowers "grow" up from behind a low curtain or imitating birds flying by). If some of the children are unaccustomed to this type of free expression, it can be helpful to let them perform their activities from behind a half curtain, so that they are hidden, or only partly visible, as in a puppet theater.

Make it clear that the sounds and the movements should go together—so if in winter someone on the "stage" is skating, the sounds should be those of skating, or if there is a tree swaying in an autumn storm, there should be storm sounds to go with it. The children should design and rehearse this independently, which will take them at least thirty minutes. The leader should go around the groups at regular intervals giving suggestions and tips when necessary.

If the group is unaccustomed to working in this manner, the leader can give very clear instructions: to the spring group she might say, "Through sounds and movements show that plants and flowers are coming up out of the ground and chicks are hatching." To the summer group, she could say, "Show in music and movements how warm it is and that people are swimming." To the autumn group, "Show in sound and movement that there is a heavy storm and the leaves are blowing off the trees." And to the winter group, "Show in sound and movement that there is a sharp frost, that people are skating and throwing snowballs."

The presentation of each season need not last more than one minute. If time permits, the four presentations can be given one after the other at the end of the lesson. Don't forget to hang the appropriate picture above or behind the stage for each season, as a kind of scenery.

It may be that the children need more time to find or make props for the movement game or for finding dress-up clothes. In that case it may be better to use the next lesson for a dress rehearsal and the final performances.

Older

Teens

**1 afternoon
or 3 lessons**

Musical Olympics

Age group: 10 and older

Requirements: instruments for half the children

Duration: one afternoon or three lessons

This short project can be done in three parts, or you can devote a whole morning or afternoon to it. The first part entails the explanation and formation of groups, the second part is for preparation, and the third is the competition itself.

Explanation (first lesson)

The Olympic Games are competitions between different countries in various branches of sport. For the Musical Olympics, first you have to make teams for the countries (four to six children in each) that will compete against one another in various musical forms. Write the names of five or six countries on the board (for example, the United States, England, Jamaica, China, Greece, and India). Next to each country write the names of about five children (according to their own choice). Then write the parts of the competition on the board:

1. Singing high (which country can sing the highest?)

2. Singing a song (which country can sing the most beautiful song?)

3. Playing instruments (which country can play a melodic or rhythmic instrument the best?)

4. Dancing (which country can perform the best dance?)

Ask the children to write down the names of their country's team and the four parts of the competition. They can prepare for the competition at home.

Preparation (second lesson)

First put the names of the teams on the board as a reminder. Tell them to first think up a battle cry or cheer for the team. This should be a short, rhythmic, scanning slogan that is called out several times by everyone together whenever a new part begins (for example, "America! Here we are!" three times).

Then the players have to find which members of their team can score the highest in the various contests; they do not have to do everything together. They can enter singly, in pairs, or in threes. Which member of the group can reach the highest notes/sing most beautifully/play an instrument best/dance well?

Make it quite clear that it is up to them how many people enter each part of the competition. After twenty to thirty minutes of preparation, preferably in separate rooms, the lesson can be closed with hearing the different teams demonstrate their cheers.

The Competition (third lesson)

The teacher is, of course, the judge. If you like, you can choose two musical pupils to assist you. First let all the groups give their cheer and begin with the first part: singing high. Using a melodic instrument, find the highest note sung by each team. The highest singer (country) gets three points, the next two, the next one. Mark the number of points for each country on the board.

Then comes "singing a song." First each country gives its cheer, and then the representatives of each country sing their song in the same order (give each singer a round of applause!). Again, the best singer gets three points, the next two, the next one. Record the scores on the board.

Next is "playing instruments." After the cheers from each country come the instrumentalists in the same order. The choice of instrument is completely open, and the children do not have to play an existing song or piece of music; they can also play a composition or improvisation of their own. Points are awarded as before, and then comes the final part: dancing. This too can be either an existing dance or one the group has made up themselves. The players can bring their own music, or the teacher can help them pick out some suitable dance music.

Finally, all the points are counted up and the teacher announces which countries came first, second, and third.

Card and Board Games

These last four games have been placed in this category because they can only be played with the help of cards or a board. Examples are printed and will first need to be copied, glued on a card, and cut out. Doing this requires a certain amount of preparation by the leader and by the children themselves. These games can also be played by only a few children at one time (except for the Musical Trivia game, which can be done with teams). The games, therefore, are primarily suitable for elementary music education with smaller groups or those just starting music lessons. They are not suitable for classical use, except for Musical Trivia, which is a very good game to use for a final class.

Instrument "Go Fish," Instrument Bingo, and the Musical Scale Race are learning games: the players learn the names and sounds of the instruments and the names of notes. Musical Trivia is a musical general knowledge quiz: it is a musical variation of the board game, involving knowledge of all sorts of facts about music. A whole group can play it if you are working with two teams. This game is ideal for the last class of the term!

Older   Teens

Instrument "Go Fish"

Age group: 10 and older; maximum of four players

Requirements: homemade cards

This "go fish" game uses six different quartets of instruments as "families" (see the illustrations). The illustrations should be copied somewhat larger and glued to cards of the same size.

The game is played exactly like other "go fish" games. The cards are shuffled and dealt. The players look at their cards and sort them into groups of the same family. If they have a complete set of four, these cards are laid on the table. The aim is to collect as many complete families as possible. The player to the left of the dealer begins asking the others for one of the cards she needs. The other members of each family are listed on the cards. If the other player has the card he was asked for, he has to hand it over, and the first player can ask any player for another card. If he does not have that card, he can ask the other players for a card. The player who has the most families when anyone has used up all his cards is the winner.

THE INSTRUMENT FAMILIES

String Instruments

Violin Cello
Viola Double bass

String Instruments

Violin Cello
Viola Double bass

String Instruments

Violin **Cello**
Viola Double bass

String Instruments

Violin Cello
Viola **Double bass**

101 More Music Games for Children

All Ages

Instrument Bingo

Age group: all ages; 5 players

Requirements: homemade bingo cards; 7 stones or counters for all the players; 12 instruments

The four cards on the next two pages should be copied and glued to cardboard. The cards are given out to four of the five players. Each player gets seven stones or counters to lay on the card. There should also be twelve different instruments, each with a characteristic sound. These could also be objects to make sounds with, such as an empty bottle, a teacup, a box of stones or marbles, a rattle, and so on. The twelve instruments or objects are placed side-by-side on a table: drum, bongo, tambourine, woodblock, xylophone, maraca, glockenspiel, flute, cymbals, bottle, cup, marbles.

The fifth player plays briefly on eight of the instruments in random order. The other players should not be able to see what she is playing. When the children hear the sound of an instrument on their card, they cover the picture with a stone or counter. The first to have a full card calls out "bingo!" and wins the game.

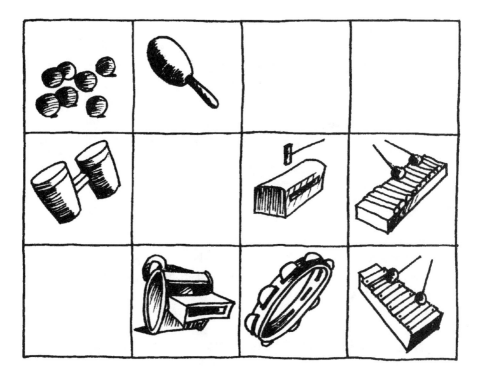

All Ages

The Musical Scale Race

Age group: all ages; groups of 2 or 3

Requirements: playing board; instrument; coin; 2 or 3 counters

Photocopy an enlarged version of the illustration of the board for The Musical Scale Race. This game can be played by several groups of two or three people simultaneously, as long as each group has a copy of the board, an instrument such as a xylophone, glockenspiel, or vibraphone, a coin, and two or three different-colored counters.

The first player flips the coin onto the instrument. If it remains on one of the bars, see which note it is and put your counter on the first space where that note appears (beginning at the bottom of the ladder). If the coin falls off, it's the next player's turn. She also throws a coin on the instrument; if she hits a note, she places her counter on the ladder, if it falls off, the next player tries. In the following round, the counter is moved to the next space for the corresponding note further up the ladder.

If a second player lands on the same note as another player, the first player's piece is "captured" and goes back to "start." The first player to reach top C is the winner.

Older

Musical
Trivia

Age group: 12 and older

Requirements: cards; counters; dice

Duration: unlimited

Copy the two pages of questions on thick paper and cut out the twenty-four cards. Make two series of six tokens out of card stock with the numbers one to six on them:

| One | Two | Three | Four | Five | Six |

Divide the class into two teams. Make sure that those players who take music lessons are evenly spread through both teams; since all the questions are about music, they have a clear advantage. The leader has the cards with the questions and the list of answers and twelve numbered tokens (six for each team).
There are six categories of questions:

1. Classical music—general
2. Jazz and blues
3. Pop music
4. World musical knowledge
5. Instruments
6. General musical knowledge

One by one, the team members throw the dice. The leader takes the first card from the pile and reads the question corresponding to the number on the dice. The teams can confer, but the one who threw the dice has to give the answer. A correct answer earns the team one token for that category and a chance to throw again. If the answer is wrong, it is the other team's turn to throw.

If someone gets a question in a category for which their team already has a token, they must answer the question first and then throw again if the answer was correct. Correct answers always mean an extra turn; wrong answers always mean it's the other team's turn. It is up to the leader to say whether an answer is right or wrong, according to the list of answers on page 160. The first team to collect all six tokens wins. There is a time limit of one minute for each question to be answered.

Variation: The six tokens with numbers can also be combined with the six letters of a word. Next to the number is also one letter from a six-letter word (thought of by and known only to the leader!) Each team has a different word. The first to guess their word when it is their turn is the winner. This makes the game shorter.

Card One

1. Which European composers are known as the three Bs?
2. Which famous jazz musician was nicknamed "Satchmo"?
3. Which is the most famous pop group of all time?
4. What musical style from the Caribbean did Harry Belafonte make popular with his recordings of "Day-O"?
5. To which family of instruments does the violin belong?
6. How many beats does a whole note have?

Card Four

1. In which century did Mozart live— 16th, 18th, or 20th?
2. In which century did jazz begin— 18th, 19th, or 20th?
3. When did punk rock become popular— the 50s, 60s, or 70s?
4. What instrument from Trinidad was made from discarded oil barrels?
5. What instrument is made from an inflatable animal skin?
6. Is a waltz in 2/4, 3/4, or 4/4 time?

Card Two

1. What is the leader of a large orchestra called?
2. Fill in the blank: "It don't mean a thing if it ain't got that ____."
3. Where does the term "pop music" come from?
4. What stringed instrument from India did the Beatles sometimes use?
5. How many strings does a guitar have?
6. What is the most commonly used key in Western music?

Card Five

1. Which famous composer had twenty children?
2. Who was called "The Empress of the Blues"?
3. What popular musical style of the 90s uses mostly rhythmic speech?
4. Which of these words describes the instruments in an Indonesian orchestra— taiko, woodwinds, or gamelan?
5. Name the three most important instruments in a rock group.
6. What is an étude?

Card Three

1. Who composed *The Four Seasons?*
2. Who composed "Summertime"?
3. Whose career took off after he sang "You Ain't Nothin' but a Hound Dog"?
4. From what country does the bossa nova song "Girl from Ipanema" come?
5. What is the difference between a keyboard and a piano?
6. How many lines does a musical staff have?

Card Six

1. Who wrote "Für Elise" and "Moonlight Sonata"?
2. Which jazz group became famous for "Take Five" and "Blue Rondo a la Turk"?
3. Who composed "Blowin' in the Wind"?
4. From which country does reggae come?
5. What are the instruments in a string quartet?
6. In a written piece of music, what does *"ff"* mean?

Card Seven

1. Who wrote over 100 symphonies, including *The Surprise Symphony, The Clock Symphony,* and *The Toy Symphony*?

2. What famous jazz singer wrote and sang "God Bless the Child"?

3. Who is the lead singer of the Rolling Stones?

4. Which term describes a Mexican band made up of trumpets and strings—salsa, mariachi, or cumbia?

5. What is the main difference between a grand piano and an upright?

6. Complete the sequence of solfege syllables—do-re-mi-__ - __ - __ - __ - __ .

Card Ten

1. Which Austrian city was an important center of classical music?

2. Which Southern U.S. city is often called "the birthplace of jazz"?

3. In which English city did the Beatles get their start?

4. From what country does the didjeridoo come?

5. What is another name for the penny-whistle?

6. What does SATB stand for in a chorus?

Card Eight

1. Who wrote the "Unfinished Symphony"?

2. What instrument did Benny Goodman play?

3. Which group sang "Surfin' USA"?

4. In which country would you hear jigs, reels, and hornpipes?

5. What is the name of the instrument in which the sound is produced by hitting wooden bars of different sizes?

6. What is the musical term for playing notes short and detached?

Card Eleven

1. What instrument did Vladimir Horowitz and Artur Rubinstein play?

2. What instrument did Fats Waller and Art Tatum play?

3. What instrument does Elton John play?

4. What is the name of the African instrument in which metal keys are plucked by the thumbs?

5. What instrument was named for the Italian terms loud and soft?

6. How many keys do most pianos have?

Card Nine

1. Who composed the opera The Magic Flute?

2. What is the style of jazz from the 1920s called in which several instruments improvise at the same time?

3. What style of rock did the group Metallica play?

4. From which country does flamenco come?

5. What is the main instrument used in flamenco music?

6. How many 16th notes are there in one beat?

Card Twelve

1. What famous composer wrote the well-known song "Lullaby"?

2. Which famous ragtime piano player wrote "The Maple Leaf Rag"?

3. In which rock group did guitarist Jerry Garcia play?

4. From which continent can we trace the roots of musics as diverse as blues, jazz, samba, salsa, and calypso?

5. What is the name of the double bell used in Brazilian samba?

6. How do you spell the word used to describe the patterns of time in music?

Card Thirteen

1. What is the name of the choral piece by Handel that is traditionally sung at Christmas?

2. What is the name of the first written blues composed by W.C. Handy?

3. What style of pop music did The Temptations, Smokey Robinson, and others sing?

4. What country does the folk song "Sakura" come from?

5. What American instrument derived from an African model became popular in bluegrass bands?

6. What does *allegro* mean?

Card Sixteen

1. How many movements are there in a piano or violin concerto—1, 2, or 3?

2. Which band's signature tune was "Take the A Train"?

3. Which megastar became famous for the dance steps known as the "Moonwalk"?

4. What is the name of a popular Mexican song about a cockroach?

5. What instrument is associated with Christian heaven?

6. What does *presto* mean?

Card Fourteen

1. Name a famous ballet by Tchaikovsky.

2. What famous trumpet player changed his style many times during his forty-year career?

3. What group of three musicians became well-known in the 50s and 60s for reviving interest in folk music?

4. In which country might you hear a tarantella?

5. Which instrument was invented by Adolphe Sax?

6. How many flats are there in the key of F?

Card Seventeen

1. Which two 19th century composers were married to each other?

2. Who played a trumpet with the bell faced upward and helped create Latin jazz with his tune "Manteca"?

3. Which rock group became known for the Latin tune "Oye Como Va"?

4. Which great salsa timbale player wrote "Oye Como Va"?

5. What is the name of the Cuban instrument made up solely of two sticks?

6. What is it called when notes are accented between beats?

Card Fifteen

1. What is the popular title for opera stars Luciano Pavarotti, Placido Domingo, and Jose Carreras?

2. Who was the American saxophone player who helped Brazilian bossa nova become popular in the United States?

3. Who was the most popular American male singer in the 1940s?

4. Who was the most popular French singer known for her rendition of "La Vie En Rose"?

5. What is the name of the Cuban drum played in Latin, rock, and jazz bands?

6. What does *crescendo* mean?

Card Eighteen

1. Which famous Asian cello player has recorded several styles of music both inside and outside of the traditional classical repertoire?

2. What was Charlie Parker's nickname?

3. What was the name of the group that sang Bob Dylan's "Mr. Tambourine Man"?

4. What is the most popularly sung-about bird in many European folk songs?

5. What instrument plays the bird in Prokofiev's *Peter and the Wolf*?

6. What is the highest instrument in the woodwind family?

Card Nineteen

1. What famous cartoon film did Walt Disney make about well-known pieces of classical music?
2. What old film featured singer Lena Horne and jazz pianist Fats Waller?
3. The Beatles made films named for some of their songs. Name one of them.
4. What was the name of the movie and recording featuring elderly Cuban musicians?
5. What is the largest drum in an orchestra?
6. What is unaccompanied singing called?

Card Twenty

1. Saint Saëns composed a piece about animals. What is its name?
2. Which trumpet player won a Grammy in both the jazz and classical category?
3. Who achieved popularity with his song "Don't Worry Be Happy" and also sings in jazz groups, conducts symphonies, and creates his own vocal pieces?
4. Which American guitarist has recorded with African, Indian, and Cuban musicians?
5. Which two instruments in the orchestra have references to a country in their name?
6. What does a dot after a quarter note mean?

Card Twenty-one

1. What is the name of the period of music in which Chopin, Schumann, and Liszt wrote?
2. What is the name of the style of jazz created by Charlie Parker, Dizzy Gillespie, and others in the 1940s?
3. What is the name of the style of vocal back-up that was used by many rock and roll groups during the 1950s?
4. In what country would you hear scales called "ragas"?
5. What is the special pedal used for electric guitars called?
6. How many measures or bars are used in standard blues?

Card Twenty-two

1. Which Russian composer wrote "The Rite of Spring" and "The Firebird"?
2. Many jazz musicians had "royal" nicknames. Name one.
3. Which famous female rock star starred in the movie "Evita"?
4. Name the type of music played by traveling Jewish bands at weddings and celebrations.
5. What are the enormous drums in Japan called?
6. What is the name of the five-note scale considered to be the most universal scale?

Card Twenty-three

1. What piece by Ravel repeats one melody over and over?
2. What is the form of a jazz standard like "Satin Doll"?
3. Which two singers sang "Bridge Over Troubled Waters"?
4. Which style of music in Louisiana came from French migrants from Nova Scotia?
5. Which instrument doubles as a percussion instrument and a tool for washing clothes?
6. What are the three most popular chords (by number) in Western folk music?

Card Twenty-four

1. Name a famous female African-American opera star.
2. What famous jazz singer began her career with a hit version of the children's song "A Tisket A Tasket"?
3. Who is nicknamed "the King of Soul"?
4. What is the name of the Middle Eastern goblet-shaped drum?
5. What is a violin bow made from?
6. What does pizzicato mean?

Answers

Card One
1. Bach, Beethoven, and Brahms
2. Louis Armstrong
3. The Beatles
4. calypso
5. strings
6. four beats

Card Two
1. conductor
2. swing
3. popular music
4. sitar
5. six or twelve
6. G

Card Three
1. Vivaldi
2. George Gershwin
3. Elvis Presley
4. Brazil
5. keyboards are electric
6. Five

Card Four
1. 18th
2. 20th
3. the 70s
4. steel drum
5. bagpipe
6. 3/4

Card Five
1. Bach
2. Bessie Smith
3. rap
4. gamelan
5. drums, bass, guitar
6. a study

Card Six
1. Beethoven
2. The Dave Brubeck Quartet
3. Bob Dylan
4. Jamaica
5. two violins, viola, and cello
6. *fortissimo* (very loud)

Card Seven
1. Haydn
2. Billie Holiday
3. Mick Jagger
4. mariachi

5. strings are vertical in an upright piano and horizontal in a grand piano; upright is smaller
6. fa-sol-la-ti-do

Card Eight
1. Schubert
2. clarinet
3. The Beach Boys
4. Ireland
5. xylophone or marimba
6. staccato

Card Nine
1. Mozart
2. Dixieland
3. heavy metal
4. Spain
5. guitar
6. four

Card Ten
1. Vienna
2. New Orleans
3. Liverpool
4. Australia
5. tinwhistle
6. soprano, alto, tenor, bass

Card Eleven
1. piano
2. piano
3. piano
4. thumb piano—also kalimba and mbira
5. piano or pianoforte
6. eighty-eight

Card Twelve
1. Brahms
2. Scott Joplin
3. Grateful Dead
4. Africa
5. agogo
6. r-h-y-t-h-m

Card Thirteen
1. *Messiah*
2. "St. Louis Blues"
3. Motown
4. Japan
5. banjo
6. lively

Card Fourteen
1. *The Nutcracker Suite* or *Swan Lake*
2. Miles Davis
3. The Kingston Trio or Peter, Paul and Mary
4. Italy
5. saxophone
6. one

Card Fifteen
1. The Three Tenors
2. Stan Getz
3. Frank Sinatra
4. Edith Piaf
5. conga
6. increasing in loudness

Card Sixteen
1. three
2. The Duke Ellington Orchestra
3. Michael Jackson
4. "La Cucaracha"
5. harp
6. fast

Card Seventeen
1. Robert and Clara Schumann
2. Dizzy Gillespie
3. Santana
4. Tito Puente
5. clave
6. syncopation

Card Eighteen
1. Yo Yo Ma
2. Bird
3. The Byrds
4. cuckoo
5. flute
6. piccolo

Card Nineteen
1. *Fantasia*
2. *Stormy Weather*
3. *A Hard Day's Night* or *Help!* or *Yellow Submarine* or *Magical Mystery Tour*
4. *Buena Vista Social Club*
5. musical
6. *a capella*

Card Twenty
1. *Carnival of the Animals*
2. Wynton Marsalis
3. Bobby McFerrin
4. Ry Cooder
5. French horn and English horn
6. three eighth notes or adds a half beat

Card Twenty-one
1. Romantic
2. Be-bop
3. doo wop
4. India
5. wah-wah
6. twelve

Card Twenty-two
1. Stravinsky
2. Count Basie or Duke Ellington or Lady Day or King Oliver or Empress of the Blues [Bessie Smith]
3. Madonna
4. Klezmer
5. Taiko drums
6. pentatonic

Card Twenty-three
1. "Bolero"
2. AABA
3. Simon and Garfunkel
4. Cajun
5. washboard
6. I, IV, V

Card Twenty-four
1. Marian Anderson or Jessye Norman or Kathleen Battle
2. Ella Fitzgerald
3. James Brown
4. dumbek or darrabuka
5. wood and horse hair
6. pluck the string instead of bow it

The Games Arranged According to Age Groups

Young Children

2. Melody or Rhythm?
4. What Animal Was That?
9. Telegraph Game
10. Instrument Quiz
13. The Chain of Sound
15. The Mosquito
16. Sound Game
18. Watch Out for Your Number!
19. Who's Got It?
24. The Triangle
28. Play Like an Animal
29. Musical Conversation
32. Find Your Own Instrument
34. The Playground Game
43. Musical Fish
44. Word Clapping Game
45. Name Game
46. Start and Stop
47. Before and After
48. Fast or Slow
49. Drumming
51. Guessing Game
68. Dance to the Sign
87. Orchestra Game
88. La Pulga de San Jose: Latin American Song with Movements
89. Circle Game from Curaçao

Young and Older Children

5. Symphony of Syllables
8. Repetition Game
21. Let Sleeping Dogs Lie
25. Telephone Game
39. Train Game
53. Rhythmic Orchestra Game
56. The Tree of Sound
57. Dead-End Street
58. The Racetrack
66. The Standing Dance
67. Stick Dance
77. The Underwater Journey
78. A Springtime Walk

Older Children

11. Living Memory
12. The Chime Bar Game
35. Sound Riddle
50. Find Your Own Rhythm
55. Song Rhythm Game
61. Body Music
83. The Multicultural Circle Dance
84. Multilingual Canon
85. Multicultural Song Festival
86. An English and Turkish Fox
92. The Impossible Task: A Moroccan Sound Story
93. Circus Project
94. Fairground Project

Older Children and Teenagers

Teenagers

All Ages

More SmartFun Books

SmartFun Activity Books *for ages 4 and up encourage imagination, social interaction, and self-expression in children. Games are organized by the skills they develop. Simple icons indicate appropriate age levels, times of play, and group size. Most games are noncompetitive — they encourage and reward children for participating, not for winning — and require no special skills or training. Many games are good for large group settings, such as camps, birthday parties and day care, others are easily adapted to meet classroom needs. The series is widely used in homes, schools, day-care centers, clubs, and summer camps.*

All books are available in paperback ($14.95) and spiral binding ($19.95).

101 MUSIC GAMES FOR CHILDREN: Fun and Learning with Rhythm and Song
by Jerry Storms

This lively and imaginative book is being used to help children learn about music  and sound while they develop the ability to listen, concentrate, be creative, improvise, and trust one another. All you need to play these 101 music games are music recordings or CDs and simple instruments, many of which kids can have fun making from common household items. Children and adults get to play listening games, concentration games, musical quizzes, and more. No musical knowledge is required.

Translated into 11 languages worldwide!

160 pages ... 30 illus. ... FOR AGES 4 AND UP
Paperback $14.95 ... Spiral bound $19.95

101 MORE MUSIC GAMES FOR CHILDREN: New Fun and Learning with Rhythm and Song *by Jerry Storms*

This action-packed compendium offers song and dance activities from a variety of  cultures. The easy games help children enjoy themselves while developing a love for music. Besides listening, concentration, and expression games, this book includes rhythm games, relaxation games, card and board games, and musical projects. *101 More Music Games for Children* can be part of any basic musical training program, either in the home or in school. A multicultural section includes songs and music from Mexico, Turkey, Surinam, Morocco, and the Middle East.

176 pages ... 78 illus. ... FOR AGES 6 AND UP
Paperback $14.95 ... Spiral bound $19.95

101 LANGUAGE GAMES FOR CHILDREN: Fun and Learning with Words, Stories and Poems *by Paul Rooyackers*

 Language games are effective tools for teachers who want to improve their pupils' communication skills. **Part One** explains the value of language games, how to choose and plan a game for a particular setting, and how to motivate players. **Part Two** describes 101 language games, most of them for children ages 4 to 16.

   The games range from simple letter games and sensory games that teach young children words for sensations and feelings, to telling jokes and advanced word play, story-writing games, and poetry games including Hidden Word and Haiku Arguments.

144 pages ... 27 illus. ... Paperback $14.95 ... Spiral bound $19.95 ... FOR AGES 4 AND UP

More SmartFun Books

101 DANCE GAMES FOR CHILDREN:
Fun and Creativity with Movement
by Paul Rooyackers

The games in this book combine movement and play in ways that encourage children to interact and express how they feel in creative fantasies and without words. The games are organized into meeting and greeting games, cooperation games, story dances, party dances, "musical puzzles," dances with props, and more. No dance training or athletic skills are required.

160 pages ... 36 illus. ... FOR AGES 4 AND UP
Paperback $14.95 ... Spiral bound $19.95

101 DRAMA GAMES FOR CHILDREN:
Fun and Learning with Acting and Make-Believe *by Paul Rooyackers*

Drama games are a fun, dynamic form of play that helps children explore their imagination and creativity. These noncompetitive games include introduction games, sensory games, pantomime games, story games, sound games, games with masks, games with costumes, and more. The "play-ful" ideas help to develop self-esteem, improvisation, communication, and trust.

160 pages ... 30 illus. ... FOR AGES 4 AND UP
Paperback $14.95 ... Spiral bound $19.95

101 MORE DANCE GAMES FOR CHILDREN:
New Fun and Creativity with Movement
by Paul Rooyackers

Designed to help children develop spontaneity and cultural awareness, the highly original games in this book include Animal Dances, Painting Dances, Dance Maps, and Dance a Story. **Dance Projects from Around the World** include Hula dancing, Caribbean Carnival, Maypole, Chinese Dragon Dance, and Brazilian Capoeira.

176 pages ... 44 photos. ... FOR AGES 4 AND UP
Paperback $14.95 ... Spiral bound $19.95

101 MORE DRAMA GAMES FOR CHILDREN:
New Fun and Learning with Acting and Make-Believe
by Paul Rooyackers

The selection includes morphing games, observation games, dialog games, living video games, and game projects. A special **multicultural section** includes games on Greek drama, African storytelling, Southeast Asian puppetry, Pacific Northwest transformation masks, and Latino folk theater.

144 pages ... 35 illus. ... FOR AGES 6 AND UP
Paperback $14.95 ... Spiral bound $19.95

101 IMPROV GAMES FOR CHILDREN AND ADULTS *by Bob Bedore*

Introducing the next step in drama and play skills: a guide to the magical art of creating something out of nothing, using skills you didn't know you possessed. This book explains the basics of improv, the "dos" and "don'ts" of performing, and how to teach improv to children. Exercises include instructions on what to watch for and avoid, and how to know if you are succeeding. The games include freeze tag games, emotional games, fairy tales, guessing games, and narrative games. A wonderful resource for educators, drama students, or the layperson looking for fun. Also contains advanced improv techniques and tips for thinking on your feet.

192 pages ... 65 photos ... Paperback $14.95 ... Spiral bound $19.95 ... FOR AGES 5 AND UP